DOLLARS AND SENSE

The Teen-Age
Consumer's Guide

DOLLARS AND SENSE

Elizabeth McGough

illustrated by Tom Huffman

William Morrow and Company
New York 1975

Library of Congress Cataloging in Publication Data

McGough, Elizabeth.
    Dollars and sense.

    SUMMARY: A factual guide to many consumer problems encountered by teen-agers when making large purchases, looking for work, and applying for credit.
    1. Youth as consumers—Juvenile literature.   2. Finance, Personal—Juvenile literature.   3. Consumer education—Juvenile literature.   [1. Consumer education.   2. Finance, Personal]   I. Huffman, Tom.   II.   Title.
HC79.C6M3   640.73   75-19109
ISBN 0-688-22046-0
ISBN 0-688-32046-5 lib. bdg.

For Michael, Steven, Mark, and Tim,
who have shared their consumer experiences with me.

Contents

Introduction

You, as a teen-ager, belong to the most powerful group of consumers in the United States. The more than forty million of you between ages thirteen and nineteen spend over twenty-four billion dollars a year. Small wonder then that industrial and retail sellers cast an eagle eye on the youth market.

Although you as a group make up only 20 percent of the population, you account for over 40 percent of record sales, 55 percent of soft-drink sales, 55 percent of movie-ticket sales, and more than 40 percent of camera sales. You buy 40 percent of all sporting goods and at least 35 percent of all cosmetics.

This tremendous buying power should give you added advantages. With all these producers, advertisers, psychologists, and market researchers competing for your attention, you have a very real influence on consumer products from clothing and music to automobiles and breakfast foods. But who decides what you want? You are constantly bombarded with pressures, invitations, and urgings from every possible medium—from radio, television, magazines, newspapers, and direct mail. Do you buy what you want or need? Or do you buy what advertisers insist you must have for the image you hold of yourself?

The spending habits you develop as a teen-ager often continue throughout life. Some people feel cheap not to "buy the best" or the most expensive product available. We may think having an expensive item gives us a better image, higher status with our peers. Here's an extreme case of peer influence on buying. Fourteen-year-old Steve commented, "I don't want to buy these cheapie sneakers. I'd be embarrassed. My friends will laugh at them if they're not Converse."

Did he choose the sneaker because he needed it or out of insecurity that he might be ridiculed if he bought an unknown brand? Consider this popular notion: Many people think that only the limited-income buyer chooses lower quality products. They may believe that a high-income, well-educated consumer always buys the best. Not so! In fact, many research studies confirm that the better educated, high-income buyer actually buys more carefully, evaluates, and shops around after he learns as much as possible

about the quality of products available. He also resists advertising pressure more than the low-income consumer. Generally the lower-income, less-educated buyer buys on impulse, pays a higher price, and prefers the more expensive, though not always the best quality, merchandise. He gets less value for his money, often gives in to advertising or salesman pressure, and is more apt to buy on installment.

Much research—plus lessons from personal wounds—has gone into preparing this book. A questionnaire was given to more than five hundred students to determine what facets of money use interested them most. Surprisingly, many wanted to know what it costs to run a home. How to get a job and how to understand the law were also areas of high interest. What the students wanted to know has influenced the organization of this book.

Young people often seem chagrined at their treatment in the marketplace, where many feel they are not treated as well as adults. Apparently a teen-ager needs to be armed with the very best consumer information when he ventures into the market maze.

This book is designed to be a reference when you need special information about advertising, credit, or how to buy something. It can pay for itself the first time you read it through. It may also start you off on money-saving techniques that will serve you the rest of your life.

To bring some order to this vast territory of personal consumerism, I have chosen to begin with a brief look at money problems and finding a job, then a hard, cool appraisal of advertising, followed by an examination of health frauds, supershopping, credit, buying a car, the law, and how to complain effectively.

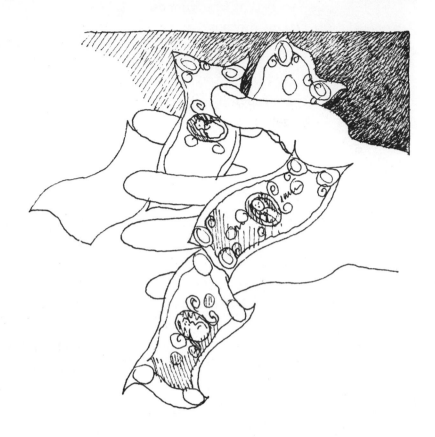

A fool and his money are soon parted.
ANONYMOUS,
current since sixteenth century

1

Do You Have
Money Problems?

If you think you have money problems, then you are not alone.
Money, or the lack of it, is a basic concern in our society. We often
measure success in terms of earning power. Money and the ability
to earn it help put us on the road to independence.

Allowance

Young adults usually have at least one stable source of income,
their allowance. *Webster's Dictionary* says an allowance is "Something given regularly to a dependent for a specific purpose." An
allowance is temporary, something like a crutch to prop you up
until you can stand on your own legs. What you learn from an allowance may be a vital key to your money management as an adult.

Perhaps you have complained, "But my allowance isn't enough.
All the other kids get more than I do." A common complaint, to be
sure. Yet allowances are often expected to do different things. You
may get a four-dollar weekly allowance, and your best friend may
get eight dollars. But her allowance may have to cover school

lunches, school supplies, bus fare, music lessons, and clothes, while yours may be intended to cover only snacks and recreation.

Two teen-agers in one family bragged that they put their entire allowance in a savings account. Yet they were given money for a movie anytime they asked and were handed money daily for snacks, music lessons, and any possible need. The allowance was, in fact, a family way of saving. It certainly gave the young people no experience in handling money.

The basic purpose for giving you an allowance should be settled by the time you are a teen-ager. If you and your parents agree that the allowance should cover only extra things, luxuries, then you would likely settle with your parents on a smaller amount. If the allowance is intended to help you learn to be a responsible spender, it will cover a wider range of expenses and would need to be larger.

A Budget

When you approach your parents for a discussion of your allowance, you'll need to be armed with some information about your expenses. You'll need to know clearly what your actual expenses are and exactly what you spend your money on. The simplest way to gain this information is to keep a notebook.

Get a small notebook that you can carry in your pocket. Write down everything you buy or spend money for, whether it's bus fare, a milkshake, a birthday gift, or a school notebook. At the end of each week, transfer these notes to a larger ruled notebook, in which you should make columns for each category of expenses. Snacks, school supplies, recreation, or grooming might be headings.

In another section of your notebook, list all your income. Include allowance, gifts, and part-time or occasional jobs. Then compare your income with your outgo. When you have kept such records for a month, you'll have a clear picture of where your money goes. Now circle all impulse spending with a red pencil. Or if you seem to spend too much money on snacks, circle those items. If your school supplies tally too high, you could bring up the problem when you discuss the need for an increased allowance with your parents. Possibly your needs are more than you originally estimated. You can show your notebook as evidence. You may see where you should change your spending habits. You may decide to give up a daily snack to save for a concert ticket next week. A budget should keep you from spending wastefully. It should help you plan your spending so you can enjoy it more.

Fritzi, seventeen, has been budgeting her money since she was fourteen, a high-school sophomore. Fritzi explains, "I get seven dollars a week, but that has to cover everything. That includes school needs, clothes, cosmetics, recreation, and savings. My mom helped me work out the budget, but it was my idea. I've really learned a lot by keeping to a budget." Fritzi now has a part-time job to supplement her allowance. Her job earnings paid for her car and now pay for gasoline, car insurance, and any other car expenses. She has determined that she will save at least one half of her paycheck and that fifteen dollars per month is her maximum clothing allowance. Before Fritzi had a part-time job, she did not need a car. Thus, her seven dollars weekly allowance was budgeted:

School supplies—.25
School lunch—.50
Clothing—$3.50
Christmas club savings—$1.00
Entertainment—$1.00
Miscellaneous—.75

Since Fritzi sews many of her own clothes, she managed easily on her clothing budget. She feels budgeting has made her far more conscious of values in her shopping. "Sometimes my mom would buy an outfit that cost twenty-five dollars, and after I wore it once, I just didn't like it, so I wouldn't wear it. When the money comes from your own pocket, you can't afford to buy on impulse or something you feel so-so about." From the miscellaneous account, Fritzi bought her cosmetics. She rarely purchased snacks, since she felt she could get them at home without using her allowance. Baby-sitting or helping with the housework brought in money for special things, such as guitar lessons or gymnastics.

In contrast to Fritzi, Steve, fourteen, earns about forty dollars a month on his paper route, yet he has no idea where his money goes. "I'd really like to go on the school ski trips, but I can't afford them," Steve moaned. "I'd like to go to Sacramento next summer to visit my old friends, but I can't seem to save any money," Steve continued. From his regular income of forty dollars, Steve saved sporadically. Sometimes he put twenty-five dollars in his savings account. Then, for several months, his money slipped through his fingers. He made no major purchases, had no expensive hobbies. "Where does it all go?" Steve wondered. He knew that a great deal of his earnings went for snacks and food away from home, even though his parents gave him seventy cents daily for school lunches. His parents paid for all clothing, school supplies, and sports equipment. His earnings were strictly for his own pleasure or for special wants. He bought an occasional record, went bowling or to a movie about once a month.

Reluctantly Steve began to keep a notebook on his spending habits. After basketball practice, he always downed two large cokes—fifty cents gone. At the school store, he bought gum and

candy nearly every day—another twenty-five cents. Steve stopped at a hamburger drive-in at least once a week, at the cost of over one dollar. At the shopping center, Steve again bought something to eat or drink. His notebook quickly added up to nearly five dollars in snacks per week. He was eating up his profits. He also found that he bought more records than he had realized. Anytime he wandered near the record shop, he bought "just a couple of cheapies." The

cheapie records cost one dollar each, and he bought two each time
he stopped. In a month he had a total of six, plus one more expensive album. Clearly, if Steve wanted to ski or save money for a trip,
he would have to change his spending habits. He decided to work
out a systematic plan that would include regular savings, a new
bike fund, and limited snacks.

A budget that works for one person may not be adaptable for
another. As one consumer advocate comments, "Each of us should
learn to spend our money by the characteristics of our own circumstances."

There are three ingredients in the good life:
learning, earning, and yearning.
CHRISTOPHER MORLEY

2

Jobs, Anyone?

The United States Department of Labor recently said, "Summer jobs can be found virtually everywhere." But they aren't being handed out on street corners. You need quite a bit of hustle and some know-how to find a summer or part-time job.

Where do you begin? Finding a job is a job in itself. Recognize this fact before you start looking. Take a close look at the classified ads in your local newspaper. Some jobs available to you may be listed under part-time jobs. Some newspapers list jobs only alphabetically, under the specific job open. Try all your sources, including friends who work, relatives, neighbors who may own or operate a business. Stop in at restaurants, stores, lumber yards, nurseries, or drive-in restaurants. For an industrial job, call the personnel office and request an appointment to talk about employment. Plan what to say when you make the initial contact.

Suppose, like Becky, you have one year of typing and you'd like a summer job. Where could you possibly find one? An insurance office, a department store, or an industry might need summer help

17

while regular employees take vacation. Becky called three places before she found one that might be interested in her services. She said, "May I come in for an interview?" When she was told they'd like to see her, she asked, "When would be a convenient time?" "Tomorrow, Thursday, at 10:00 A.M.," she said, repeating the time back to the employer.

What Is a Résumé?

For the interview, Becky dressed neatly and simply in a summer dress, with stockings and small-heeled shoes, not sandals and bare legs. She took a neatly typed résumé with her. The résumé summed up her qualifications, telling these facts: Who am I? What do I know? What have I done? What kind of work do I want? Why should I be hired?

Here's a sample résumé that Becky prepared:

NAME:

Rebecca Welch

ADDRESS:

1920 Placer Drive, Fair Oaks, California 95628

PHONE:

783-6427

PERSONAL:

Sex: Female

Height: 5′ 5″

Weight: 110 lbs.

Date of birth: May 1, 1960

Health: Excellent, no physical limitations

EDUCATION:

Hanford Junior High

Will enter Hanford Senior High, September 1975

Honors and School Achievements:

   Honor student, B+ average, Junior High

   President, Debate Club

   Secretary, Student Body

   Certificate:

      Outstanding Junior-High Language Student

SKILLS:

Typing, 50 wpm

Knowledge of cash register and adding machines,
   learned in school store

Can operate mimeograph and ditto machines

Speak and read Spanish fluently

EXPERIENCE:

Have worked in school store 2 semesters

Baby-sitting, 3 years

Helped prepare school newspaper

School office, typing

Candy striper, Mercy Hospital, volunteer work

HOBBIES, CLUBS, INTERESTS:

Gymnastics

Skiing

Youth Guild, Westside Lutheran Church

REFERENCES:

Mrs. John Curran, 108 Oak Place, Fair Oaks, California
(Baby-sat for Mrs. Curran)

James Davin, 112 Tenth Street, Sacramento, California
(Typing Teacher)

Mary Jennings, 1970 Sheridan Street, Sacramento, California
(Volunteer Chairman, Mercy Hospital)

JOB DESIRED:

Typist

Office helper

File clerk

Becky's résumé gave the prospective employer something visual to consider after the interview. Preparing it gave Becky a chance to think through what her assets were as they would apply to this job. A résumé is thought to be one of the most effective job-hunting tools and can often precede the actual interview. By sending a well-prepared résumé to possible employers, you may "get your foot in the door" and obtain an interview. A résumé can help you put facts together that will increase your self-confidence, and you can avoid underselling yourself when you take stock of your achievements. One high-school business class had excellent training in preparing a résumé. More than 70 percent of the students trained in office skills had jobs lined up before they graduated.

Pounding the Pavement

While a résumé can be an effective tool for landing many jobs, some jobs require really imaginative thinking and sheer resourcefulness in order to discover them. What jobs might be open to you, a teen-ager with little experience and limited skills? For one thing, as a teen you have a few assets many adults do not. You have lots of time and a high energy level. Think of some chores that adults don't get around to doing: garage cleaning, weeding, seasonal garden chores, window washing, refinishing or painting a porch or deck, floor waxing, car washing, hedge trimming, and snow removal. You can probably think of a dozen more. What else could you do? House sitting while neighbors vacation, lawn watering, dog and plant sitting are other ideas. Party help, including serving and cleanup, offers a good chance for a teen-ager, boy or girl, to earn money.

Kim and Sharon, both fourteen, typed up small slips of paper, advertising their desire to find part-time work, and passed them out to their entire neighborhood. They said: "Two hard-working teen-agers, Kim Stannard and Sharon Brown, want jobs. We will: specialize in party help, help prepare hors d'oeuvres, serve, clean up; organize birthday party games, serve, clean up; baby-sit and entertain your children, day or evening. Both experienced, reliable, with references. Call: 967-0332 or 967-8888.

Kim and Sharon were overwhelmed with calls and soon had regular customers who counted on them to help with summer and holiday parties. They worked hard, particularly at birthday parties for children, and they charged a fair rate. For evening parties they were paid at least $1.50 per hour for each girl, while the hostess enjoyed her guests. The girls poured water in glasses on the dinner table, served appetizers, set out food when they were instructed to, cleared cocktail glasses while guests ate, and cleaned up completely, including the washing of some large pans and silverware by hand. Mrs. Stone commented, "For less than ten dollars, I can enjoy my company and not face a mess the next morning." Working as a team, one girl could care for young children while the other helped with early evening serving.

Where else can you find a job? Restaurants and diners want kitchen help, waitresses, busboys, janitors. Carhopping at a drive-in restaurant is a popular teen job. Community recreation centers need cashiers, clerical help, concession-stand workers, craft instructors, groundkeepers. Banks and insurance offices need clerical help, mail and messenger help, coin wrappers, typists. A car wash and a gas station may need help, and a summer theater may need stagehands and sign painters. A pet store may hire you to bag pet litter or feed the animals and fish. A golf course needs more help in the summer to pick up driving-range balls and to retrieve balls from water hazards. Grocery stores hire teen help as stock clerks, bag boys or girls, and cleanup for in-store bakeries. Doctor and dental offices may need vacation help for phone answering, filing, record keeping. Politicians and charity offices want help to stuff envelopes, address mailers. Amusement parks and zoos often need part-time help.

Don't overlook these other job sources: Can you sew? Why not sew for pay? Advertise your skills either by a flyer delivered in person or by word of mouth through friends and acquaintances. A nursery or day-care center may need help with small children, and another type of nursery may need help with landscaping, watering plants in warm weather, repotting, digging plants, and carrying purchases to cars. Arts-and-crafts or gift shops are usually willing to take articles on consignment, keeping a percentage of the asking price for selling them. Tutoring in reading, math, or a foreign language can bring income for a resourceful teen. What other skills do you have? Could you organize a lesson group for painting, craft, knitting, needlework, tennis, swimming, or piano lessons? Are you good with mechanical things? Perhaps you could offer to change or rotate tires, wash cars, drain antifreeze for pay. If you can drive a car, you may offer to do errands or deliver children for swimming or piano lessons.

No skills, just willing to work? Here's a job many either overlook or turn up their nose at, yet there's a tremendous demand for it. Housecleaning pays well, and you won't have trouble finding work. Kathy, now seventeen, finds this job great for her needs.

"I'm through by two in the afternoon, so I have plenty of time for my own fun. At first I kind of cringed at cleaning for people. I bought some rubber gloves to use in bathrooms. That's the only part I minded anyway. Vacuuming, dusting, cleaning a sink, wiping down kitchen cabinets isn't that bad, and most people are so glad to have you that they are happy to pay two dollars or more an hour. I work four days a week in summer, and I earn at least ten dollars a day. During the school year, I have one regular Saturday job that pays fifteen dollars for six hours." When Kathy first began housecleaning, some customers expected her to watch children while she worked. She explained that she couldn't, and since she had more jobs than she could take, she could easily eliminate customers who expected too much. As with any job, reliability is a key factor in housework. Many people earn up to twenty dollars a day cleaning either homes, apartments, or hotel/motels.

Orchard and agricultural work also offer employment opportunity for young people. In many areas, orchardists offer a one-day training program for pickers. They may also give out schedules showing approximate dates when each crop will be ready, where help is needed, and rate of pay, usually based on the quantity harvested. Some teens have earned sixteen to twenty dollars a day harvesting cherries, peaches, and apples. Orchardists employ teens to help sort and grade fruit in warehouses. Canneries also offer employment during the harvest season.

Manpower, Inc., a major employment agency, has founded Youthpower, Inc., an agency to find jobs for young people, with no fee to the job seeker. In 1972, Youthpower found jobs for 10,000 young people. Youthpower has free training clinics where experts put you through a brief, but intensive course to prepare you to work at a job where you've had no prior experience. Check in the yellow pages of your local phone book to see if such an agency exists in your community. Other agencies may also place temporary help, loaning you out to any place that needs your skills. The positions can range from delivery help to clerical work.

Another plus for a teen who wants to enter the labor force is that you need not let the money offered deter you. You may find that an interesting job or one that gives you special experience suits you better than one that pays well. For example, you may want a closer look at a possible career opportunity. You may work in a hospital, a library, a social agency, or in a laboratory doing something related to a career you are considering. Volunteer work can give you wide experience that may aid in future paid jobs. Teen-agers have worked with the mentally retarded, with senior citizens, and with church or community recreational programs in many parts of the country. An official of Manpower, Inc., commented, "Young people who participate in these programs are representative of the fact that everything which is done does not necessarily have to have a dollar sign hung on it. They make a contribution to their community, but they're also widening the scope of their education, an investment in their future."

Volunteer work may lead to paid employment, as it has done for several California students who worked at a center for the mentally retarded of all ages. Some volunteers eventually decided to pursue a career in social work or in speech therapy. Jan, sixteen, explained, "You feel good about what you are doing, even though it can be frustrating at times. So much can be done to help. . . ."

Michelle thought she might like to be a nurse, so she sought a summer job at a hospital. After working there for three months, she said, "I don't think nursing is for me. I plan to find something else for a possible career field."

Government Jobs for Teens

For the older teen, from about sixteen to nineteen, summer jobs do exist within Federal agencies. They vary from jobs in the Youth Conservation Corps to working in the halls of power in Washington, D.C., for a specific office or official. Barbara, seventeen, worked as a tour guide in the public-information office of the Voice of America. She earned $430 per month. Gary, eighteen, worked at a Youth Conservation Corps camp tackling such problems as cleanup around polluted rivers and helping preserve historic sites. Many jobs offer room and board and a small salary. Each year a *Summer Employment Directory of the United States* is issued. Most of these jobs are in summer camps, resorts, hotels, restaurants, and ranches where the pay may be as low as $200 for someone with few skills to offer. National Park Service sometimes employs young people as guides, living-history interpreters, or as arts-and-crafts demonstrators. If you live near an area administered by the Service, apply to the park superintendent for such a job. The United States Government also gives a Civil Service Summer Employment Exam, and you must apply not later than January each year to take the test in March. You may write to Summer Employment Examination, U. S. Civil Service Commission, 1900 E St., NW, Washington, D.C. 20415. You may also call the Federal Job Information Center in your area, listed under United States Government, and ask for Announcement 414 for details about this examination.

Lawful Limits on the Job

Are you limited by law in what type of work you may do, or in what hours you may work? You are indeed. Last summer, Mike, fifteen, worked for the greenskeeper at a new golf course. He started working at 6:00 A.M. and finished at six in the evening, when

he fell exhausted into bed. He wanted the job badly, so he told the
employer, "I can't work such long hours every day." His boss replied, "Says who?" Mike finally quit. Had he been aware of the
law, Mike could have kept his job. The Fair Labor Standards Act
does not allow a fourteen- or fifteen-year-old worker to work more
than eight hours on nonschool days. This age group may work at
jobs under the following conditions:

Outside school hours: not before 7:00 A.M. or after 7:00 P.M.
   (9:00 P.M. from June 1 through Labor Day)
3 hours on school days, to a maximum of 18 hours during school
   weeks
40 hours on nonschool weeks
8 hours on nonschool days

A sixteen- or seventeen-year-old may work at any job other than
those covered by Nonagricultural Hazardous Occupations Orders.
You must be eighteen to work in a nonagricultural job that has
been declared hazardous, such as logging and sawmill work, roofing
and excavation operations, coal-mine operations, and many occupations using power-driven machinery.

If you are under sixteen (or sometimes eighteen), you must obtain a work permit or employment certificate. Procedures vary from
state to state. Typically you call your State Department of Labor
and ask them to send you an application for a work permit. Take it
with proof of your age to your school counselor or principal for
signature and for a statement that you can handle a job during school.
Your parents or legal guardian must also consent to your working. In
some states you need a letter from the employer stating the conditions of your job. Then you need a new certificate for each new

job. Or the form may be issued for a stated period of time and can be used for more than one job. An employer who violates child-labor laws can be fined. Permits are not required for harvesting fruit, yard work, baby-sitting, household work, or caddying.

The Job Interview

Now you have some idea of where jobs can be found, how to write a résumé, and legal restrictions. But what about that moment of truth, the personal interview? You won't get a job through the mail or over the phone, that is, by being an armchair angler. You must get out and see people yourself. Some interviews may be the initial contact, as when you call on a small shop or business to ask for a job. Others may be formally arranged. In either case, here are some guidelines to follow:

1. Apply alone and don't take friends along for moral support.

2. Gather together in an easily accessible order all information you may need to take with you: work permit, Social Security card, proof of age, school records, résumé. Carry it in a folder or large envelope.

3. Be on time, or even a little early.

4. Know what you have to offer, what you can do, and what kind of job you want.

5. Be ready to furnish references, not related to you, by name, address, and business. Ask them in advance if you may use their names. They should know your work and your character.

6. Allow as much time as may be needed for the interview. Don't be concerned about a prearranged time for someone to pick you up.

7. Dress conservatively, not too formal and not too casual, but appropriately to the type of business.

8. Be neat, clean, have your hair combed, fingernails trim and clean, shoes shined.

9. Each interview may be different, yet each gives you a chance to present yourself to the best possible advantage. Be natural and try to be at ease. When you are asked to sit down, sit comfortably without slouching. Don't throw your arm across the back of a chair.

10. Let the employer control the interview. Give complete answers, brief, without rambling.

11. Look directly at the interviewer. Don't stare at your feet or at the door, as though you wish to escape. When you meet someone's eyes directly as you talk, you are thought to be honest, sincere.

12. Thank the employer for the interview. Write a follow-up note when you get home.

Here's a sample letter you may use:

> Street Address
> City, State, ZIP Code
> Date

Mr. James Smith
The Camex Corporation
110 Madison Avenue
Pittsburgh, Pennsylvania 15212

Dear Mr. Smith:

I would like to thank you for the time you devoted to my interview with you and for the courtesies extended to me. I am interested in the job you described and would like to be an employee in your company.

If there are any other questions that I may answer, please feel free to contact me. I look forward to your decision.

> Very truly yours,
> Name

When you apply for a job, be sure that you complete the application carefully and correctly. Steve, sixteen, applied for a job at the J.C. Penney Company recently. On the application, under Type of Work Desired, he wrote in, "Full Time." He actually wanted part-time work during school and full-time work for the summer. The employment manager mistakenly thought this applicant planned to drop out of high school, and his application was passed over. Steve later contacted the employment manager when he found friends who had applied later than he were being hired. After the error in application was changed, Steve had a job as a salesclerk in the men's department.

Social Security and Income Taxes

When you join the labor force, you should apply for a Social Security number. You can obtain a form from your State Department of Labor.

On Steve's first regular part-time job he earned $2.25 an hour. "I was surprised at the bite taken out of my check for taxes and Social Security," he said. The Social Security deduction is not refundable, but you can get a refund on any income tax that is withheld as long as you haven't earned more than $2,050 in one year. Your employer is required to send or give you a statement of earnings, a W-2 form, about one month after the year ends. If the Government owes you money, file a tax return, Form 1040, to get a refund of your taxes paid. If you earned over $2,050, you *must* file a tax return. Or, if you are still a dependent of your parents and have gross income of at least $750 and any of it comes from unearned income (dividends, interest), you must file a return. Is there a limit on your earnings while your parents declare you as a dependent? No matter what you earn, if you are still dependent upon them for more than half of your total upkeep, they can claim you as a tax deduction until you are nineteen or longer if you are a full-time student for at least five months of the year.

If you had no tax liability the previous year and expect none this year, you can file Form W-4 E to escape allowing your employer to take that bite out of your paycheck. To get this form, phone the nearest Internal Revenue Service Office and ask them to mail it to you. Don't forget, though, if your employer has already withheld tax money, file a tax return at the end of the year to get that money back.

Teens are income producers, and according to the 1970 census 58 percent of boys and 48 percent of girls between ages fourteen to nineteen earned an income. The median income for boys was $685; for girls it was $491. The number of students employed in October, 1971, was double the level employed in the early 1960's. In the sixteen- to nineteen-year-old range, 77 percent of girls and 68 percent of boys worked at part-time jobs sometime during 1970. (United States Department of Labor, Monthly Labor Review, August.) The United States Department of Commerce has an interesting booklet called, *We, The Youth of America,* June, 1973, which you can obtain for forty cents by writing the Superintendent of Documents, U.S. Government Printing Office, Washington, D.C. 20402. This booklet shows the types of jobs young people hold, how many work, how many are married, on the move, voting record, etc.

Would you like to join the labor force? As you can see, you have to "sell" yourself to an employer. One employment counselor commented, "Finding a job takes finesse, know-how, and persistence. Don't be easily discouraged."

For three consecutive months
they could barely afford
the most unnecessary luxuries of life.
NORMAN DOUGLAS

3

The Great Advertising Game

"Today is your lucky day," Sandi's letter read. "You have won a free stereo. To collect your prize, simply present this letter to the address shown below." Sandi read the letter again carefully. When she went to collect her "prize," the salesman pointed out one ambiguous sentence that meant she would have to join a record club before she could claim her stereo.

Reluctantly she agreed. The salesman then abruptly guided her to another part of the store. "Just let me show you this really fine stereo—a much better product. The stereo you get free has parts that are tough to replace. You have to ship it to a factory for repairs. For just a few dollars a month, you can enjoy first-class stereo with your new records."

In less than an hour after she had gone to collect a "free" gift, Sandi had bought an expensive stereo that she hadn't intended to buy. She had also joined a long-term record club for records she could have bought more cheaply elsewhere.

Don't laugh! Such little dramas happen every day. Perhaps you know someone who has been taken in on such a scheme. Bait and switch happens often in the sales jungle. A fantastically cheap product (the bait) lures you into a store, with a come-on that sounds too good to be true. It is! When you get there, a salesman assures you that you wouldn't be happy with this cheap tape recorder, stereo, sewing machine, or whatever. For only a few dollars a month, you can have an excellent one. Or, in another bait-and-switch routine, you are told that the advertised product is sold out.

All bait-and-switch practices aren't quite so blatant as the one Sandi encountered. Sometimes the ad merely creates a false impression of the quality, size, or style of the product, even though the true facts are later made known to the buyer. This type of bait

and switch is still a violation of the law, if the first contact with the prospective buyer is made by deception. The primary purpose of such an ad is to lure you into the store.

Deceptive sales tactics appear in many disguises, even though the purpose is always the same: to trick you into thinking you are getting more for your money than you really are. Your best line of defense is to shop around before you buy that fantastic bargain. Yet the marketplace isn't getting any simpler. One United States senator estimates that Americans lose more than *$200 billion* dollars per year through various anticonsumer practices.

Much advertising serves a useful purpose of telling you the things you need to know about merchandise. Some informative advertising is excellent, such as the ads in a Sears, Roebuck mail-order catalog.

These ads describe the product and help you distinguish the various models of it. Many ads, though, appeal to your emotions, your image of yourself, often because the advertiser's product and a competitor's product are essentially the same.

Many great commercial ventures exploit young people. Companies try to sell you anything from posters and notebooks to records and clothing by using a peace symbol. They imply that by buying their product you are somehow endorsing peace.

Economists estimate that from 20 to 40 percent of the cost of any product is spent on advertising. That's your money that is being spent. When you buy a widely advertised brand of toothpaste or shampoo, it may have been manufactured on exactly the same production line as the store's own less expensive brand of the same product.

A useful type of advertising is the sale ad that tells you when merchandise is on sale in certain stores. A department store may lower the price of seasonal clothing late in the season, or it may have traditional months for sales on certain items. Ski and winter sports equipment may go on sale in February, while bathing suits and summer clothes go on sale in July. (See chart *When to Buy What* on pages 86-87.)

Sale!

Sale ads can be misleading, unless you read carefully and know something about the vocabulary advertisers use. Here are some common terms used in ads:

Regularly $99.95, now $69.95. This means that after the sale, the regular price returns, assuming the store is honest about its claim of the normally higher price.

List price. A manufacturer puts this price on the box, often so the retailer can make you think you are getting a bargain by selling it for less. Few stores actually sell at the list price.

Fair-trade item. This means that the item is sold at this fixed price everywhere.

Comparable to $99.95 value. An ad may indicate the merchandise is comparable to higher-priced goods, but this claim may only be the opinion of the store owner.

Below manufacturer's costs. No manufacturer is in business to lose money, so ask yourself why would anybody sell goods below cost? Did the product turn out to be a poor seller? Are parts no longer available for it?

Seconds. A small flaw exists such as a pulled thread or unmatched design. Such a flaw may affect the wear of the garment or goods.

Irregulars. According to the Federal Trade Commission, irregulars have only very minor defects that will not affect wear. Towels and sheets are often sold this way at much lower cost than first-quality items. Sweaters and jeans are also sold this way. When buying either seconds or irregulars, you should look the product over carefully to determine if the reduced price is worth having the flaw.

As is. Merchandise may be missing some part, or it may be chipped, torn, or broken. If you buy goods in possibly soiled or stained condition, there is usually a substantial reduction in price.

Special purchase. These goods may be below the store's usual quality, but also may be a good buy. Or a store may buy out a manufacturer's style that is being discontinued.

Pitfalls in the Marketplace

Let's look at some of the more common pitfalls in the sales jungle known as the marketplace:

Deceptive advertising: Products are sometimes advertised at reduced prices when, in truth, they were never sold for the higher price. "New, low price" the ad might read. Be wary of such ads.

Contests, surveys, free goods: "Hi! Is this Dan Jones? It is, well, great," the exuberant voice bubbles on. "If you can answer one very simple question, you may receive the most fantastic tape-recorder offer ever made. Are you ready? Now listen carefully. Who was the first president of the United States?"

Dead serious, the caller waits for your answer. Believe it or not, thousands of so-called contests are conducted by phone every week, peddling photographs, magazines, beauty offers, etc. Some callers even skip the contest routine. They just say, "You have been chosen as the lucky winner of. . . ." To claim your "prize," you must pay or sign a contract to pay at least the total value of your prize. The fee may be disguised as a delivery charge, membership fee, or the cost of some companion item that goes with your prize. A record club might go with a phonograph; an expensive service policy or sewing course might go with a sewing machine.

Be wary of such a come-on. Thousands of people are tricked by deceptive techniques into buying things they later regret. No one is in business to give things away. By the time we reach our teens, we realize exactly what we get for nothing. Nothing! Yet the age-old lure of something free proves irresistible to many of us.

Doorstep salesmen: Everything from magazines to silverware and pots and pans finds a way to your doorstep. The lifetime warranty for the $200 set of pots and pans will be small comfort when the company or salesman cannot be located two years later. High-pressure tactics, including the pitch, "Your friend Joan asked me to show you this set. If you just take a few minutes of your time, she will receive, absolutely free, a beautiful transistor radio." Well, who

can resist for a friend? But don't buy his wares. Girls often start a "hope chest" in their teens, and they are particularly susceptible to such salesmen.

Magazines bought at the doorstep have a habit of never appearing. The publisher often has no record of your subscription. When you subscribe to a magazine, do so on a bill-me basis. Pay the bill after you receive your first issue.

Chain-referral schemes: "Why shouldn't I buy this $200 typewriter? It's too good a deal to pass up. It will hardly cost me anything in the long run, because I get commissions for each friend who will buy one," Mike explained to his doubting parents. Every year thousands of people end up paying exorbitant prices for popular items, including cameras, television sets, stereos, and household appliances, because they are lulled into believing that an unlimited market exists for "this wonderful new idea in product X." In most cases, the victim is lucky to earn even one or two commissions. He is stuck with an item he cannot afford to buy at half the price. Such offers sometimes appear on your doorstep, although many come through the mails.

Mail-order sales: According to the Federal Trade Commission, mail-order selling tops the list of consumer gripes. You order and pay for something. The merchandise never comes. If you complain to a reliable firm, you will usually get satisfaction. Know the company you deal with.

Is there any way to get off mailing lists, so you won't receive so much junk mail? Yes, you can write to Consumer Relations Manager, Direct Mail Advertising Association, 230 Park Avenue, New York, N.Y. 10017, and ask for a name-removal form. By signing and returning this form to them, you'll be taken off all lists that belong to the Direct Mail Advertising Association. This organization covers about 65 percent of direct mailers.

If you want to get on mailing lists, you can write the same association. You can request that your name be placed on mailing lists for clothing, sporting goods, or specific items that may fall in the realm of their advertising members.

In either case, one should be aware of the pitfalls involved with buying by mail. Perhaps a flashy ad for a tape recorder arrives. The price: a mere $49.95. You can buy it at a discount house for $42, however. If you pay in the suggested six monthly payments, the extra cost of $8 is equal to 55 percent true per annum interest.

There are several basic types of mail-order firms. Some are quite reputable and useful, including such major mail-order houses as Sears, Roebuck, Montgomery Ward, and J. C. Penney Company. They offer wide variety, good service, current styles, and easy exchange if you are not satisfied. Still, you often pay the same price that you would pay in a local discount or department store.

Novelty mail-order houses often advertise in glowing, breathless terms for the clever, ingenious, cute, amazing, handy items that they carry. Their ads sharply contrast with the factual, straightforward ads of major mail-order firms. Some of these items may strike you as just what you need or want. Yet most of the useful ones in these catalogs can be found in local stores for less money. Others are cheaply made and poorly designed, as well as misrepresented in ads. Many of the goods in these pamphlets, often attached to Sunday newspaper supplements, are planned to appeal to the impulse buyer, the uncritical shopper.

Mail-order wishbooks often make buying addicts out of us. As an experiment, a group of consumerism writers went on a buying spree. Each thing they ordered arrived within a few weeks, and refunds were made promptly. Then what could they complain about? Here are a few examples of their purchases: A super salad maker was easy to clean and to operate, as the ad said, but the gadget to make "creative masterpieces" did not cut, chop, or slice food uniformly. It merely *tore* the food apart!

A three-dollar pocket saw was a total waste of money. It did cut very thin wood but only scratched glass. The saw was actually a silicon steel thread looped between two rings and was advertised to cut plastic, ice, bone, brass, steel, etc. After attempts to experiment with it, the saw broke into five pieces!

A $12.50 surprise box contained an assortment of unimpressive

items, including a cheap necklace, five gold-plastic picture frames, a four-page photo album covered with cardboard in a wood-grain design, a consumer handbook, an ounce of cheap perfume, and four other useless things. Such surprises may have added up to over twelve dollars in retail cost, but who would want this horn of plenty?

All of the items ordered proved to be disappointing, even though technically some of them did the job the ad claimed they would do. One miracle-mending powder was supposed to make repairs undetectable, to end sewing, mending, weaving forever. It did indeed mend the nylon ski jacket the experimenters tried it on. A sticky blob on the jacket, though, was not exactly invisible.

Buying from a foreign firm: Many American magazines carry ads for foreign goods, from Norwegian ski sweaters to sandals or jewelry from Israel. Send a letter of inquiry by airmail, and most firms will send you a catalog or letter stating costs and postage in American dollars. Send a check when you order. Any goods bought abroad are subject to duty, and the postal service will send your package through customs inspection when it arrives. Small packages of modest value may be duty free, but if the customs officer decides to charge you duty on your package, he will attach a bill to the package. This duty is usually about 20 percent of the value. You pay your local mailman. You may be pleased with a good buy.

Unordered merchandise: If unsolicited merchandise comes to you, you aren't obligated to pay for it. Free samples must be clearly marked as such. Charitable groups may mail merchandise to solicit funds. In either case, you may consider the merchandise as a gift if you like. It is illegal for the firm to bill you, says the FTC. If you are plagued with requests for payment, write to the FTC, Washington, D. C. 20580. If you receive unordered goods, you can:

1. If the package has not been opened, write "Return to Sender" on it and put it back into the mail.

2. If the article is not wanted, set it aside for a reasonable period of time and, if unclaimed, destroy.

3. Treat it as an unconditional gift.

Book and Record Clubs: In a questionnaire given to more than five hundred high-school students, the top complaint involved record clubs. "I order and pay for records, and they never come until I write threatening letters," was a common story. While buying records through a record club seems appealing initially, doing so can become a burden. Record clubs typically offer ten records for one dollar each as an incentive to join. The agreement you make when you join may obligate you to purchase at least six records in the coming year at the club's regular price. The regular price is claimed to be a bargain. But, in fact, the club price may be the same that you would pay at a local store or more than you would pay at a discount mart. When buying through a record club, you also pay postage and handling charges.

Some record clubs require you to mail back a notice before a certain date or that month's selection will automatically be sent to you. If you are slow in mailing, or misplace the notice, you may receive a $5.98 selection you don't want. In that case, you can write "Refused" on the unopened record and place it in the mails. Do not pay in advance for any record or album you order.

Some record clubs have cheaper quality recordings or tapes than you would want. Be sure you know what quality records are offered before you sign a membership agreement.

Book clubs operate in much the same way. The initial offer is attractive. Then you buy books at or slightly below retail list price. You agree to buy a certain number of books during the next year. You also pay postage and handling of perhaps eighty cents to one dollar per shipment. Unless the book is one you will use repeatedly, you may be just as happy borrowing it from the library for the one time you intend to read it. Popular books are also available in paperback after they have been on the market for about one year.

False claims, earn-at-home variety: There are many earn-at-home ways to help you make a fruitless investment of time and money. Home study and other school ads sometimes falsely say their graduates earn enormous salaries. Such ads may also say that big name professionals personally guide your course, critique your work. In most cases, you receive standard comments at various stages in the course. The pros lend their name for a fee. You would be wise to look for a similar course in your local community at either a vocational school or a community college.

A classified ad appeared in many newspapers in the United States offering women a chance to earn up to $1.68 an hour sewing baby shoes in their own home. More than 200,000 inquiries were made. Each prospective sewer had to pay a small registration fee and demonstrate her skill by sewing a pair of wool felt shoes for infants. In this particular scheme every one of the 60,000 job applicants failed to measure up to the promoter's high standards.

Photo-coloring schemes are also common devices used to fleece victims out of money. Glowing ads lure you with the hope of earning over two dollars an hour by working in your spare time in your own home. You pay a fee for a kit to start with. Then all of your work is rejected as not up to quality.

One of the most vicious traps the consumer today faces is the high-pressure promoter who launches a campaign promising high-paying jobs for anyone who signs up for his training program. The course may be in nursing, computer programming, or heavy-equipment operation. It costs several hundred dollars and can be purchased on credit. Thousands of people respond to the campaign, send in checks for down payments, and sign a contract to pay the rest. They report for training. The training turns out to be totally inadequate to equip them for the promised jobs. Or the "school" has skipped town. The promoters have sold the contracts to a finance company, paid off themselves, and filed for bankruptcy.

Jean, sixteen, dropped out of high school. She read the promise of "guaranteed job as a licensed practical nurse" by taking a correspondence course. Sharon was attracted to the exciting, high-paying job of an airline stewardess that the sales pitch described. Both girls signed a contract for total payments adding up to several

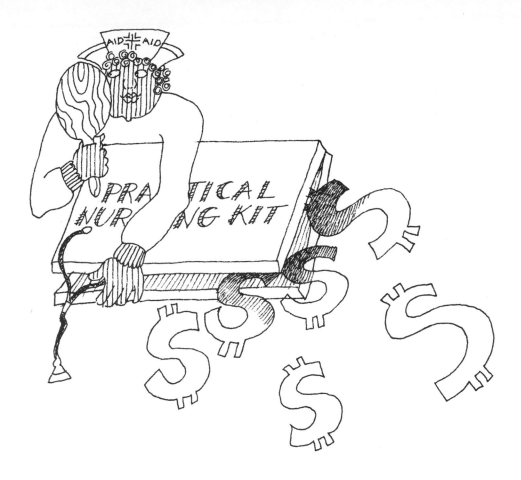

hundred dollars over an extended period of time. Each girl received an impressive-looking diploma, but neither one was adequately trained for the job she wanted. Before buying a correspondence course, check with employers in the industry involved to determine its value. You may also write to your State Education Department or to the Bureau of Higher Education, U.S. Office of Education, Washington, D.C. 20202, for information on the school.

Animal schemes for quick profit: Have you ever been tempted by an ad that said, "Earn thousands of dollars in your spare time by raising chinchillas (or nutrias, or minks). Small investment." Rais-

ing such animals is a highly specialized job with tremendous pitfalls
for the inexperienced. Some companies offer a buy-back plan, after
you have bought expensive breeding stock. They claim they will
buy back the offspring and that the breeding rate is prolific. You
can easily part with your money this way, while promoters earn
high profits. Many such ads misrepresent actual facts.

Vanity press: *Vanity press* is the term used to describe the group
of publishers who flatter and promise you fame and fortune if you
let them publish your book or poetry. Such publishers may also
refer to themselves as *subsidy publishers.* The inexperienced, fledg-
ling author is particular prey. His creation may have been rejected
by several reputable publishers. Then, when things look darkest,
the vanity press seems to offer exactly what he is looking for—
praise, promise, and a balm for his bruised ego, in the form of a
contract to publish his book. The catch? You pay a substantial advance, from five hundred to several thousand dollars—an investment
in your book, they say.

Beverly, a high-school senior, was delighted that her children's-
book manuscript won first place in a local writing contest. She tells
this story: "I read a glowing ad for a subsidy publisher, complete
with testimonials from authors who had allowed the company to
publish their book. So I sent the one-thousand-word manuscript off
to New York. In a few weeks, I received a handsome folder including a contract, telling all the advantages of having the company
publish my book. In the contract they asked for one thousand dollars
as an initial payment to put the book into production. One afternoon
I got a phone call from Hollywood! Imagine! I was really excited.
But, of course, I didn't have enough money." The publisher contacted her repeatedly in the following months. Later Beverly talked
with her English teacher. He told her she was lucky not to be taken

in by such a scheme. He suggested she go to the library to look in *Writer's Market* for a listing of possible publishers. He also told Beverly that often good manuscripts are rejected many times before they are sold.

Since publishers receive thousands of manuscripts, they rarely criticize them. You might ask an English teacher, a librarian, or a schoolteacher to read your manuscript to give you a critical opinion before you send it to a publishing house.

Indeed, the vanity publisher does print your book. He may or may not, though, live up to promises to advertise and promote your work. If you have a book or manuscript of any kind that you feel is publishable, send it to a legitimate publisher. You may not hear what you'd like to hear, but you won't be cheated either. According to the National Better Business Bureau, when the author pays, the merit of his work is not very important.

Song sharks operate much like the vanity publishers. They may lure you with the promise of having a popular vocalist record your song. You pay for the publishing costs, then find the promotional efforts are almost nonexistent. Legitimate companies do not buy words without music or expect you to pay to be published.

Advertising exerts a powerful influence in our lives. Although many ads do give a true picture of a product, many people still mistrust what they read in advertising. In 1970, an extensive study showed that 49 percent of people interviewed felt that advertising was mostly lies, that it was not at all helpful. A tremendous revolution is going on. Consumers now refuse to accept whatever Madison Avenue dictates. As part of this consumer revolt, the Federal Trade Commission has become a far more vigilant watchdog over advertising and marketing than it once was.

A company may say, "This candy tastes super," without fear of FTC criticism. But when an ad says, "Lose weight by eating two slices of this bread before a meal," then the FTC can ask the company to prove its claim. Such a claim was indeed made by a bread company. The ad did not say that you must then eat less during the meal. Another bread ad boasted that its bread has fewer calories than other breads. In fact, the bread was sliced thinner to cut calories. The would-be dieter could save five calories by eating the smaller slice of bread.

Susan was trying desperately to stick to her diet to lose weight when she heard the bread claims. "That sounds neat," she confided. "I'll try it." Of course, she lost no weight by eating two extra slices of bread. Believe it or not, she insisted that she would eventually lose weight this way—after all, the ads said so. After much prodding from a friend, Susan called her doctor to check on the claim before she would give up on it as an effective way to lose weight.

The FTC not only tells advertisers to stop using deceitful ads, they order such advertisers to tell the public they have been misinformed. This admission of wrongful ads must be carried in future advertising for that product. It cannot be done by printing a separate retraction or correction.

Although we have a giant watchdog (the FTC) on the scene to help us, the best watchdog of all is an informed, *alert* consumer.

What we sell is hope.

4

Beauty Aids, Health, and Nutritional Quackery

The ten-*billion*-dollar-a-year cosmetics industry claims, "What we sell is hope." A rather shocking price to pay for hope! Teen-agers spend an estimated $450 million each year on cosmetics, creams, and lotions. Yet cosmetics are not labeled to tell the American consumer what she buys in that five-dollar, elegant pedestal jar. We are told, "Create an oasis for dry skin." "Create the look of alive skin— a shimmering face, four ounces, $10.00." But what are we buying?

Almost since Adam and Eve man has rubbed oils and creams on the skin to soften or cleanse it. The Greek physician Galen is credited with the discovery of cold cream around 150 A.D. A mixture of olive oil and beeswax with as much water as the potion would hold, it was called "cold cream" because when placed on the skin, a cool feeling was achieved as the water evaporated. The oil and wax also provided a cleansing action by melting on contact with warm skin to loosen dirt, oil from the skin pores, and dead skin cells. This material could then be wiped off along with the cream. For fragrance, rose petals were added.

49

Modern creams have the same purpose as those in ancient times, even though science and technology have made giant strides in developing synthetics and new ingredients. Today cleansing creams may contain oil, wax, and water, in varying proportions depending on the job that they are intended to do. Cleansing creams designed to remove makeup have high oil content, while moisturizing lotions contain more water.

Even though moisturizers may all have a similar basis, prices are certainly not similar. According to one interested legislator, "Most of us know that the five-dollar jar of cream will do no more than the fifty-cent jar." Yet we buy it on the outside chance that it's more effective, thinking that high-priced things are better.

Why do we spend so much to buy superficial beauty? The cosmetics business is one of moonbeams and stardust. If we feel attractive, that feeling gives us security, makes us feel accepted and poised. But we should recognize that cosmetics cannot change us permanently, they cannot make us over, they cannot insure instant happiness. All they can do is give us a lift, brighten our best features, and help cover some of our flaws.

Fine lines caused by dryness can be temporarily de-emphasized by using a moisturizing cream. But preparations placed on the skin can't remove wrinkles caused by repeated overexposure to the sun or by aging. Baking in the sun hastens skin deterioration. Have you ever seen a young man who works outdoors all of the time? His leathery skin, though bronzed, has deep permanent creases and has aged prematurely. According to Dr. Cyril March, Professor of Dermatology, New York University, "Nothing, short of plastic surgery, can remove deep creases and wrinkles in the skin." No known product can help the skin regain elasticity and thickness, since as the skin ages it loses elasticity and becomes thinner and drier. A

drugless cream patted on unbroken skin can't reach subsurface skin tissue.

The skin is made of three layers. The outer layer, or epidermis, is composed of cornified, or hard, cells stacked one on top of another. The dermis, or second layer, is under the epidermis. It contains hair follicles, sweat glands, oil glands, along with some blood vessels and nerves. The subcutaneous layer, or third layer, is mainly fatty tissue, which serves as padding for the body. According to Avon Products, Inc., a major cosmetics firm, the epidermis cells are shed and replaced constantly from the second layer, the dermis. Although some cosmetic firms say that moisturizers can penetrate the skin's top layer, this claim is not totally accurate. Moisture, water, can be absorbed, but a cosmetic cream cannot. Some face creams contain hormones such as estrogen, and these hormones can be absorbed into the skin. They are not cosmetics, but are actually drugs.

Many home demonstrations and department stores try to sell you on a "beauty routine" that involves your buying sets of cosmetics at exorbitant prices. Or you may be offered a "free" gift when you buy a regular-size jar of an expensive item. Susan looked at a "flawless foundation" makeup base in a department store. "Why are you so reluctant to spend money on your face?" the beautiful young salesclerk asked. "After all, that's your most important asset," she urged. (According to *Seventeen* magazine, 68 percent of teen-age girls use a makeup base.) When shopping for cosmetics as shopping for anything else, resist high-pressure sales of any kind. Try a product in its smallest size, and check the price of private-label brands at discount, variety, and drugstores. Price is no criterion for effectiveness in cosmetics. Find a cosmetic that agrees with your skin at the lowest cost. If something disagrees or causes an allergic reaction, take it back. Always return something if it doesn't live up to the claim on the label or its advertising.

Drug or Cosmetic?

What makes a lotion or deodorant a drug rather than a cosmetic? If a product claims, "This deodorant makes you smell desirable," or simply states, "For lovelier skin, use XYZ hand lotion," it can be classified as a cosmetic, and the manufacturer is not required to tell you what the product contains. But if the manufacturer claims, "Stops perspiration fast, antiperspirant," then this product becomes a drug. If the product claims to change or interfere with body functions in any way, it is a drug and the company must list major ingredients on the label.

According to the Department of Health, Education, and Welfare, the law defines a cosmetic as an "article except soap intended to be rubbed, poured, sprinkled, sprayed on, introduced into, or otherwise applied to the human body for cleansing, beautifying, promoting attractiveness, or altering the appearance."

If a toilet article is offered to prevent or cure an ailment, or to affect the structure or function of the body, it is a drug as defined by Federal law, even though it may be promoted and sold as a cosmetic. Some examples are products that claim to grow hair on bald heads, to remove wrinkles, to cure a skin disease, or to treat and prevent dandruff. Hormone creams or antibiotic deodorants are defined as drugs, because their ingredients affect the function of the human body.

If the intended use of something makes it a drug, the label must give directions for use, information on composition, and warnings, if any are needed, to protect against injury or misuse.

After January, 1976, you'll no longer have to wonder just what it is you put on your skin to improve your appearance. A Food and Drug Administration regulation requires manufacturers to list ingredients in order of predominance. In certain cases the regulation will allow manufacturers to list items, then state "and other ingredients" to protect trade secrets. To do so, the company must petition the FDA for each separate product or ingredient, and the FDA will review the reasons why it should be kept confidential.

What about all the unfamiliar chemical names most of us will barely be able to pronounce, let alone know what they mean. When the label says, "contains sodium laureth sulfate," of what practical use can this information possibly be to the average consumer? Mainly people with allergies will be able to learn which ingredients they should avoid, while most people will become familiar with ingredients common to certain product groups. They will learn them by routine comparisons and normal shopping. (Sodium laureth sulfate is a cleansing and foaming compound for shampoo.) The

FDA will require a standard name for each ingredient to keep products from masquerading under a dozen names for the same thing. Lanolin oil, for example, will always be known as lanolin oil and not by any of the other fifteen names the trade has used for this substance.

Cosmetic firms argue that they would have to divulge trade secrets if they are required to list all ingredients. Yet without knowing what we buy, real comparison shopping is impossible. The Consumer Federation of America says, "Simple, inexpensive ingredients are in some cases sold to the unknowing consumer for very high prices. Knowledge on the part of the consumer is the first step toward prevention of fraud." Manufacturers also object to labeling a product by listing ingredients in the order of predominance. They do not seem anxious to let consumers know the product they buy may be mainly alcohol or water.

Are Cosmetics Safe?

"You are beautiful. I will see for you, and you will hear for me." In the *FDA Consumer*, Dr. Carl W. Bruch told this story about a deaf male college student who had just met a blind coed. She had scratched her one good eye with a mascara brush, which caused the cornea to become infected. The inflammation reduced even the slight vision she had in her "lazy eye." She was blind for a year.

The eye mascara was analyzed, and the coed learned that the temporary blindness occurred because a preservative in the product lost its effectiveness after months of storage on the store shelf. A certain type of bacteria that causes eye infections, *pseudomonas*, was found in the mascara.

While most cosmetics are safe, the National Product Safety Commission estimates that there are 60,000 cosmetic injuries a year in the United States. The cosmetic industry says this statistic is an exaggeration. Yet consumer complaints range from problems with hair dyes and tints to vaginal infections caused by bubble baths. Feminine deodorant sprays also cause complaints about burning, rashes, and other inflammations. According to the FDA, the largest classification of complaints concerns hair preparations. In 1971, they accounted for 39 percent of the total. Whatever figures are correct, the American consumer has become far more aware of product safety and of his right to complain when a product causes harm.

Sally complained that her eyes itched and burned, particularly after she had used a new frosted-lilac eye shadow. She told the doctor that she wet the shadow cake by moistening her fingertip to apply the makeup. Since eye cosmetics are an especially good medium for bacteria growth, Sally probably contaminated the product by spitting into it, then caused infection by applying it to her eyes. She had also loaned her eye makeup to a friend, who risked infection by using the shared product.

The Food and Drug Administration recommends the following tips for cosmetic safety:

1. Before using any cosmetic, read the label carefully.

2. Immediately stop using any eye product that irritates, itches, or burns. If the irritation continues, see a doctor.

3. Always wash your hands before applying eye cosmetics. Normal bacteria on your hands could, if placed in the eye, cause infection.

4. Throw away old eye cosmetics that you haven't used for months.

5. If cosmetics become dusty or contaminated, wipe off the container before using. If the cosmetic is visibly dirty, discard it.

6. Cosmetics stored in a hot car are more susceptible to deterioration. Don't store cosmetics at temperatures above eighty-five degrees.

7. Don't allow small children to play with cosmetics. Keep them out of their reach.

Hypoallergenic and Natural Cosmetics

According to Dr. Robert Schaffner of the FDA, some nonallergenic products may be accurately classified this way. The term implies that if you are allergic to some cosmetics, you can safely use this type. Yet just because a manufacturer says a product is hypoal-

lergenic does not make it so. Since allergies are so broad, something that affects one person may not have adverse effects on another. If you have allergies, the best procedure is to buy small quantities to test the product. Use a small amount of it on your arm, and leave it there for twenty-four hours. If a reaction occurs (redness, blisters, itching), then you know not to use it again.

For hair tints, straighteners, etc., do a patch test following the manufacturer's directions on one small patch of hair and scalp before using it on your entire head.

Have you heard about the wonders of mink oil, royal jelly (made only by the queen bee), turtle oil, and natural herb creamgel cleanser? Will any of these products bring romance, social acceptability, and happiness any more than products made of synthetics? Will any of these natural wonders better remove the flaws in our skin or better cover the dark circles that a sleepless night has brought? There is no proof that the many claims made by natural cosmetics are valid or that natural cosmetics are more easily absorbed into the skin. The American Medical Association suggests that consumers be wary of overstated claims about exotic ingredients. These ingredients often have no purpose except to sell the product.

Suntan Products

Sharon wanted to have a suntan look on her shoulders and back for her new halter dress that she planned to wear to the Valentine's Ball. She began using a tanning product advertised to give a tanned appearance without exposure to the sun. By the day before the dance, Sharon had a blotchy, mottled look. Some of the "tan" had worn off when she washed while other areas that were probably applied unevenly looked spotty.

The Food and Drug Administration says these products do not

seem harmful when used according to directions, even though they have received some complaints about them. Analysis of the suntan products has shown them to be perfumed alcohol-water solutions, containing dihydroxyacetone and a small amount of acetone. Dihydroxyacetone, which has for many years been used in drugs, reportedly gives the tanning effect, although we don't know how this chemical reacts with the skin. FDA experiments indicate that after several scrubbings, much of the "tan" disappears and may leave a mottled look.

Whether you burn to a crisp or tan a golden brown, you can profit by knowing a little about the myriad suntanning and sun-protection products on the market. A sunburn will never change to a tan. Anything more than a slight burn will peel the top layer of skin in a few days, and then you are back where you started. You can avoid a burn by staying in the sun for short periods each day, ten to twenty minutes, depending on your skin's sensitivity and the sun's strength. How deeply you tan depends on the amount of melanin your skin contains. Melanin is a pigment your skin provides to protect you from harmful sun rays. The sun stimulates melanin (produced in the lowest layers of skin), and it then concentrates in the outer layer, darkening to create a barrier against harmful rays.

The vast array of lotions, creams, oils, gels, and butters fall into three groups.

1. Suntanning aids moisturize your skin while you bask in the sun. They contain no sunscreen chemicals and usually don't list their ingredients on the label, other than to boast of coconut oil or lanolin. These products can counteract drying effects of the sun or wind, but can't prevent sunburn unless they have sunscreen chemicals added.

2. Sunscreen products contain chemicals that block out burning rays at the same time they allow longer ultraviolet rays to work at tanning you. Para-aminobenzoate (PABA) and homo-methyl-salicylate are effective sunscreens and are listed on the label if they are found in the product.

3. Sun-block products include zinc oxide or products that contain high amounts of PABA that could effectively prevent sunburn. Zinc oxide is the creamy white material you often see on a lifeguard's nose. Sun-blocking products usually claim their effectiveness in strong language on the label.

Acne

"You don't have to wear an acne pimple to school today"—fact or fiction? This popular ad may seem like a broken record to the troubled teen-ager with acne on his face, for seemingly everywhere he turns someone has good advice about acne. From family and friends to TV and magazines, much ado is made of teen acne. It can be a serious problem and does occur to some extent in about 80 percent of adolescents. At a time in life when a person is quite sensitive about his appearance, no one likes to face the world with bumps and blotches on his face. What to do about it and what causes acne in the first place?

Lynn described her ordeal with acne: "My mother said, 'You don't drink enough water. Maybe you need a laxative.' Aunt Mary says 'Stop eating sweets, get more sleep.' My older sister says, 'For heaven's sake, stop thinking about sex. Relax!' A teacher told me, 'You don't wash well enough. Scrub your face better.' My friend Lisa said, 'Stop eating meat. Become a vegetarian.' My brother claimed that only physically weak people get acne. My girl friend and I tried eleven different acne products, including a mint-julep facial masque, a guaranteed natural wonder super cleanup, and medicated pads. None of them worked very well, and most did nothing at all!"

In desperation Lynn went to a dermatologist (a doctor who specializes in skin care). He explained that at the time of adolescence, oil glands in the skin enlarge. Fueled by increased activity of the endocrine glands, which secrete hormones to influence parts of the body, the oil (or sebaceous) glands secrete oils that usually reach the skin surface through pores. Often, though, the oils seem to dam up back in the ducts or in the lining of the hair-follicle wall. Dead cells may store in layers and block the pores instead of allowing oils to reach the skin. The dead cells combine with oil and bacteria and form pimples, or white heads. Redness and inflammation may also result as oils continue to accumulate and work with bacterial enzymes, further irritating the hair-follicle walls. The doctor told Lynn that acne didn't come from being physically weak, or from not eating the right foods, or because she needed a laxative. Even though he did emphasize that she should wash her face with soap and warm water at least twice a day to remove accumulated oils, he pointed out that acne is not a disease of dirt. He did say that there's no instant cure for acne, but that a continuing process could help control it.

Lynn was told that no single product was ideal for everyone. Antiacne preparations come in creams, gels, lotions, soaps, medicated towelettes, and masques. Each person's skin varies in sensitivity and in the degree of acne that he may have.

Many nonprescription, or over-the-counter, aids may help, if they contain effective antiacne ingredients. According to a national consumer-product testing service, four specific medications commonly used in antiacne aids are considered effective. These active ingredients are benzoyl peroxide, sulfur, resorcinol, and salicylic acid.

If the product label doesn't list any of them or contains less than 2 percent resorcinol or salicylic acid, it's probably too weak to help you. All of these products inflame the skin and cause it to peel.

If you think certain foods—chocolate, milk, potato chips, and French fries—make your acne worse, try eliminating them for a few weeks. If the acne clears, then gradually add them back to your diet to see if your condition gets worse again. Most dermatologists feel foods make no difference.

Remember, however, that acne won't make you a social leper, just as clear skin can't guarantee social success.

Over-the-counter Drugs

Sometimes over-the-counter (OTC) drugs are advertised in such a way that you can hardly resist. Suddenly you have a problem you never recognized before, or such amazing results are promised that you'd be foolish not to reach out for the product.

Although thousands of OTC drugs are safe and will bring results for minor symptoms, such drugs should never be used regularly. Many Americans are pill poppers, taking a pill or potion for headaches, fatigue, stomachache, jittery nerves, or insomnia. But these drugs won't cure a disease even if they do relieve symptoms. If a problem persists, you should see a physician.

Always read the label on any drug that you use. Federal law says that labeling must provide all directions needed by the average person, including certain conditions under which the drug should not be taken. Follow these instructions carefully.

If you have a reaction or bad side effect to any product, stop using it immediately. Ask your pharmacist if he can recommend any similar drug for your symptoms that won't cause a side effect. If your reaction appears to be serious, consult your doctor.

Never use any combination of drugs—either several OTC drugs together or an OTC drug along with a prescription drug. A dangerous or even fatal reaction could result. Don't buy pills to pep you up or sleeping pills to calm you down. Try to find the underlying cause of fatigue or insomnia.

Drinking and drugs can be a dangerous duo. Antihistamines and sleeping pills can produce drowsiness if used with alcohol.

Any medicine should be treated with respect and should not be used lightly. They should be kept well out of reach of small children. A handbag sometimes contains easy access to enough drugs (even aspirin) to kill a curious toddler.

Organic Foods

Do you believe in the value of organic or natural foods? If you do, and you are willing to pay the high cost of these foods, do you get what you pay for? At a public hearing in New York City, testimony was given by a confidential investigator for the Bureau of Consumer Frauds and Protection that organic foods were generally priced at two or more times the price of regular foods. From wheat berries to dried apricots and cereals, the investigation showed laboratory findings contradicted label claims that these foods were organically grown, unsprayed, and contained no chemical residue. In fact, the foods contained the same small amounts of DDT, malathion, and other pesticide residues usually found in foods grown under regular conditions. If you bought cashew nuts in an eight-ounce package in the health-food store for $1.10 compared to a six-ounce package for .59 elsewhere, you may have thought you were paying for "natural organic, superior quality," as labeled. Lab findings showed these nuts contained 0.18 parts per million of a chlorinated pesticide, a not unusual finding in these nuts. Organically grown raisins contained ethion, in quantity that could be found in ordinary raisins, even though the ones tested from the health-food store cost $1.15 for sixteen ounces compared to .49 for fifteen ounces in a regular store.

Are organically grown foods better for you, as many self-styled nutritionists claim? Since organic fertilizers can't be absorbed by plants until they break down to the same elements as contained in chemical fertilizers—potassium, phosphorus and nitrogen—their use is no more effective than commercial fertilizers. In fact, modern chemical fertilizers supply the plant's needs more directly and more quickly. Organic fertilizers may also contribute to spreading certain infectious diseases, says the Food and Drug Administration.

You've probably heard that our soil has lost its vitamins and minerals and that our foods have little nutritional value. The claim is another bit of nutrition nonsense. The nutrients that promote good plant growth are added to the soil in fertilizers and our food crops do contain the expected nutritional values.

Jenny popped a half-dozen "natural" vitamin pills into her mouth every morning. "Everyone needs 'natural' vitamins to stay healthy," she explained. Vitamins are specific chemical compounds, and we use them equally well whether they are man-made or produced naturally. To help protect consumers against deceptive promotions, new Food and Drug Administration regulations say that no dietary supplement can claim superiority for either a natural or synthetic product. For example, rose hips, part of the rose blossom and a popular health-food product, cannot be promoted as a better source of Vitamin C than ascorbic acid tablets.

If a healthy person eats a balanced diet, including meat, eggs, milk products, fruits, vegetables, bread and grain products, he won't need vitamin supplements. If you have a balanced diet, vitamins simply overdose you. They are usually excreted, although in some cases overdoses can harm you. Too much Vitamin C can cause diarrhea, and excessive doses used in Russia were found to cause abortions in some women. Vitamin A in massive doses, sometimes prescribed for acne, has produced pressure in the skull that mimics a brain tumor. Vitamin A is no longer available over-the-counter in doses over 150 percent of the Recommended Daily Allowance (RDA). At this point, it is considered a drug not a dietary supplement.

Many people who try to sell health and nutrition aids, from pills and vitamins to quick cures for anything that ails you, are not nutrition experts; they are merely salesmen, guilty of quackery. The salesman or ad may tell you about a "secret remedy" and that the medical profession is trying to suppress the fantastic discovery. A miracle drug, device, or diet may offer "testimonials" to show what the product has done for others. Rely on competent authorities for true, dependable facts about health and nutrition, not on someone who stands to gain from your use or purchase of a product or a book he has written on nutrition.

Before and After Claims

From bust developers to weight-loss devices, consumers are bombarded with advertising claims that seem appealing indeed. Lisa considered the before and after photos an exercise-studio ad showed. "From size twelve to size nine in just three weeks, lose three inches from your waistline" the ad read. Lisa signed up for the program, hopeful of a trim figure for the beach scene ahead. After three weeks of exercise, she had learned better posture, but she had lost only one-half inch from her waist. According to the Federal Trade Commission, the before and after pictures used by reducing spas are often misleading. When our posture and facial expression change so dramatically, we may appear to have lost weight when we have actually only improved our appearance.

Bob, nineteen, overweight for years, decided to tackle his problem several ways. He bought an over-the-counter product to chew before each meal to suppress his appetite, and he invested in a vibrator and a "sauna belt," to be worn around the waist or hips. He looked forward to seeing the inches melt away, while he enjoyed his usual hot-fudge sundaes and French fries. After six months, Bob gave up and went to see a doctor. He learned that any massage device has no effect in weight reduction, since the device does the exercising, not the person. He was also told that nonprescription diet pills are clinically of little or no value. Like countless other dieters, he learned that only by eating less and exercising more can you lose weight.

Sharon had the typical hunched-over, pulled-in posture of many fourteen-year-old girls who consider themselves poorly endowed with small breasts. She was an easy mark for a bust-development ad in a teen magazine.

Yet a representative from the American Medical Association says that he has never seen convincing evidence that the breasts can be enlarged by any method except plastic surgery. Mark Eden Enterprises, who market a bust-development plan, say that 75 percent

of their customers are satisfied and that a study of five women showed increased bust measurement. While many researchers consider a sampling of five much too small to prove anything, chest muscles underneath the breasts and back muscles may be enlarged somewhat after exercise. The breasts themselves, which contain no significant muscle, cannot be enlarged through exercise. If you stand with shoulders back and chest out, you appear to have larger breasts than if you slump forward. A properly fitted bra, which gives support, can also add to the illusion that breast size has increased.

Americans have never had more choice in the foods they eat and the products they choose. They also have the right to informed choices, with honest rather than misleading advertising, to tell them what a product contains or what it truthfully can do. No one is dateless simply because she has bad breath, or is flat-chested, or uses the wrong deodorant. If we recognize that cosmetics and exterior remedies cannot assure happiness, we take one giant step toward better consumer habits.

The buyer needs a hundred eyes,
the seller not one.
GEORGE HERBERT

5

Super Shopper

The seventies have been called the "decade of the consumer." People no longer take just what's dished out to them. Everyone tries to stretch his money, as he learns to make choices in a vastly complicated marketplace.

From supermarket to clothing stores, you can save money and get better value if you sharpen your wits. Be a super shopper a few times, and soon you will be always. Here are some basic rules to follow. You may already know some of them, but other readers may not:

1. Compare prices before you buy whether shopping for a new coat, a camera, or skis. This consumer advice may seem to be standard, yet amazingly many of us do not follow it. Of course, don't shop all day to buy a one-dollar deodorant. But the higher the price, the greater the potential savings you can make by shopping around.

2. Make a rule never to spend over five dollars—or set your limit at ten dollars if you wish—for anything without checking the same product or service elsewhere. The identical product has a different price tag hanging on it in different places. Pick up the phone and "let your fingers do the walking." Ask for the specific department where you'd find the item you want, then list the price information given you. Study your list before you choose a store.

3. Buy from reputable stores. In the long run, they will satisfy their customers. This category includes discount houses, most of which are reputable and many of which are chain stores.

4. Check product ratings. This step is especially important when you plan a major purchase or want to find a product that is most effective for the least money. Buying guides such as *Consumer Reports* and *Consumers' Research Magazine* are available in libraries and on newsstands. Check the items you want in the recent *Readers' Guide to Periodical Literature*. Often you'll find a comprehensive discussion about the product in a magazine.

5. Negotiate the best possible price. Many prices are subject to negotiation. Ask if there's a cash price or a package deal possibility. A store may not be willing to lower the price, but they may throw in a related item. Hesitate a moment, don't be so eager to close the sale. Play it cool. Always assume a better price can be had for the asking. The best negotiator knows the approximate value of the merchandise before he gets involved.

For example, Susan was shopping for new skis in January, the height of the ski season. She knew that in another month skis would be going on sale at a reduced price. She had bought from this sporting-goods store before and had rented skis there to see if she liked skiing before she decided to buy equipment. The skis that suited her were priced exactly the same in several shops. She hesitated, looked at skis, boots, poles. Then she asked the store manager, "Do you think these will go on sale soon?" He agreed that they would likely be reduced late in the season if they were still unsold, probably in March. Susan evaluated, thought a moment, then said, "Well, could you fix up a package for me at a better price, if I buy skis, boots, and bindings?" The manager recognized the advantage of making the sale now rather than taking a lower price later, so he agreed. Susan got the skis for twenty dollars less, plus the ski poles the manager added as a bonus. Many skiers looking for new skis try out several styles and brands merely by asking for the promotion wagon at a ski area. They test skis for ease of turning, flexibility, and how well they suit the individual ski style, whether aggressive or conservative. Some ski shops will also allow you to try several models before you buy. What have you got to lose?

Many items, including sporting goods, stereos, furniture, ten-speeds, cars, and services can be negotiated. Start with a low offer (but not ridiculously low), leave room to go up and still not over-pay for the product. When you sell something, you always expect to come down a little. Don't be embarrassed to negotiate.

6. Buy good quality generally. Sacrifice quantity for quality most of the time. Don't end up with shoddy things just because they are low priced. Price doesn't always mean quality, and many variables enter into your choices. A good jacket or sweater may cost twice as much as a cheap one, but it will outlast two cheap ones. For fad items, though, you may not care about long life. Cheaper quality may do for a "streaker" sweatshirt.

7. Make use of free or inexpensive recreational and educational services. Look for free concerts, take a date to play tennis or picnic at a public park. Enroll in craft, guitar, sewing, or auto-mechanic courses offered by school and park districts. Patronize the library, plan a bike hike.

8. Take stock of what's plus and what's minus in your buying habits. What have you done well with your money? What has worked poorly? What kind of things do you buy that work out pleasantly? What skeletons are you hiding in the closet? Is there a pattern to your errors? How can you avoid making the mistakes over again?

As you can see, you need not be a miser with your money to sharpen your wits. You need only to plug holes that your money sifts through, and you'll have more left over for pleasures. Some common money leaks are: eating out too often, keeping up with your peer group, giving extravagant gifts, expensive hobbies, buying snacks, credit-card buying, expensive dating habits, and too many clothes unwisely bought. There is no need to live a Spartan existence, but recognize the real cost of what you are doing. Decide what you can afford at your stage of life. You may find that you need to curb expenses in one category to pay for your special interest. Do your own thing, but know what it costs.

Supermarketing

Can you break the code at your supermarket? If not, you are shopping wearing a blindfold! Most foods are coded to show their shelf life, the date beyond which they are unsafe to eat. The code 6121, for example, tells when a package of hamburger is likely to be spoiled. Add the first and last digit to get the month; the middle digits give the day. The code says July 12 is the deadline for this meat. Codes vary from store to store and from product to product. Ask your grocer to decipher his code for you.

Some stores now use "open dating," which can be read by anyone. The date may mean "pull date," which is the last day the store may

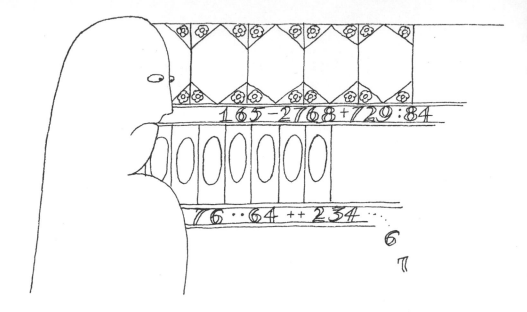

sell this item as fresh goods. The product is probably still usable for a short time to allow for home storage. But when you buy something, why not buy the freshest product available?

In one survey eighteen retail stores were monitored by a Consumer Action Committee. Ten products were watched, including eggs, milk, ground beef, and chicken. All but three stores offered merchandise that was, by the store's own standards, too old to sell. If you open a package of hot dogs or sandwich meat that feels sticky and smells strong, return it. Ask why it was sold, and ask to have the code explained.

Do you know how to read a label on a frozen dinner or on a frozen cherry pie? On a dinner, if the label reads "Noodles, chicken broth, chicken," it means that the dinner's largest ingredient is noodles, with a smaller quantity of chicken broth, and still less chicken. A cherry-pie label may say, "Cornstarch, sugar, cherries, water, etc." In this case, the pie has more cornstarch and sugar than cherries. After years of bickering between the Federal Drug Ad-

ministration and pie manufacturers, the dilemma of cherry-pie filling has been resolved. Would you believe that a Federal standard
now requires a frozen cherry pie to have at least 25 percent cherries in the filling! This regulation may seem absurd to a young
consumer, but have you ever eaten a piece of pie where you had
to search for a cherry midst the cornstarch? As you can see, what
we buy may not always be what we think we are buying. Meatballs
and spaghetti, or spaghetti and meatballs? Which do you prefer?
You may think you are buying the same thing, but think again!
The item listed first is the greater portion of the can or package.

As of December 31, 1974, manufacturers who ship products in
interstate commerce have been required to abide by new rulings
set by the Food and Drug Administration. One ruling states that
if a product makes any nutritional claim, it must carry a nutrition
statement. Even if the ad says only, "High in Vitamin C," the
product must carry complete nutrition information. The label must
show: serving size, servings per container, calories, protein, carbo-
hydrates, fat serving, and the percentage of the United States

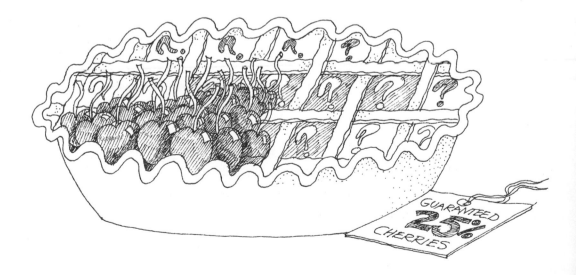

Recommended Daily Allowance (RDA) per serving for certain essential nutrients. The RDA indicates how much of nineteen vitamins and minerals is needed to maintain good health, and this amount includes leeway for body differences. Most people need only two thirds to three quarters of the RDA. If any product contains from 50 to 150 percent of the RDA, it is a dietary supplement and must be labeled this way. If it has over 150 percent of the RDA, it is an over-the-counter drug and must be labeled as such.

No product label may claim that a balanced diet of ordinary foods cannot supply adequate nutrition. Nor may a food claim that presence or absence of certain vitamins can prevent or cure any disease. A product may not claim that there is any difference between a natural vitamin or a synthetic one.

A can of Super C Orange Drink will now have to label just how much orange juice is in the product and what percentage is actually sugar water. Other labeling laws will require saying how much shrimp the shrimp cocktail contains, or how many half-cup servings of spaghetti the package has. By reading the label, you'll know what you are buying.

Unit pricing is another supermarket newcomer. Some markets tag their shelves to make price comparison easier. These tags tell you the price for a single unit of weight, measure, or count of a product. For example, Jane wanted to buy a box of cheese crackers. An eight-ounce box cost sixty-six cents, while a twelve-ounce box cost eighty cents. Instead of having to do the arithmetic in her head, the shelf tag told her the cost per ounce of each size. The eight-ounce box cost eight and a quarter cents per ounce, while the twelve-ounce box cost six and two-third cents per ounce. Not all larger size packages carry a lower price per unit, and unit pricing helps you determine those cases.

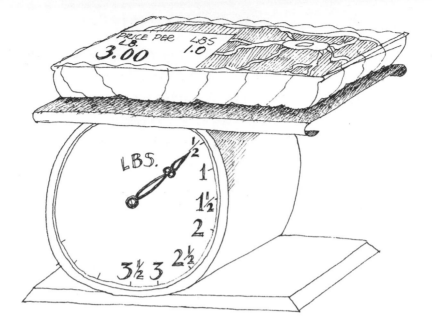

Short-weighting happens more often than many of us realize. If produce or meats are prepackaged, weighed, and priced, take the package to a scale in the store and weigh it again yourself. If a discrepancy occurs, tell the check-out clerk or the manager. The New York City Department of Consumer Affairs found 3,500 short-cutting violations in one year, and some stores were guilty of dozens of them.

When you begin shopping for a household, take advantage of Department of Agriculture aids, available for the asking or for small fees. Write or phone your nearest Agriculture Extension Service, and ask for booklets available on stretching your food dollar and on understanding nutrition. You may also write to the Superintendent of Documents, U.S. Government Printing Office, Washington, D.C. 20402, to ask for any brochures available on buying food.

In a consumerism questionnaire completed by over five hundred high schoolers, students wanted to know what running a household costs. In response to their concern, the chart on page 77 has been compiled from Department of Labor statistics.

Convenience foods and restaurant meals can also run up the food budget. Usually an already prepared food will cost more than if you do the work yourself. But the convenience of the product may be worth the cost in time and energy to you. If you are spending too much, evaluate how many convenience products you buy. Could you cut down on some of them? What are you really getting in the packaged product that you could not easily prepare yourself? If you crave beef Stroganoff, it may be easier to buy a one-serving-size, prepared main course, rather than buy sour cream, mush-rooms, sirloin steak, etc., for one person. But if the package contains mainly a starchy filler, such as rice or noodles, and very little meat, you'd be better off to prepare the meal yourself.

Lisa evaluated to see if a young couple could buy food for twenty-five dollars per week. By using eggs and cheese, and carefully watching the food budget, she felt this limit could be kept, even though she allowed one meal at a buffet-style restaurant, where they could have roast beef for three dollars per person. "If we go out for hamburgers, we spend almost that much for not nearly as good a meal," she explained. "And we don't have to tip at a smor-gasbord," she added. Tipping adds about ten to fifteen percent to a restaurant check. She also compared the cost of eating hambur-gers out or making them at home. A deluxe burger cost eighty-nine cents at a popular drive-in, a regular burger forty-nine cents, French fries thirty-nine cents, milkshakes forty-nine cents. For two people, she calculated one deluxe burger, plus a regular burger, French fries, and shake for her husband, with one deluxe burger, fries, and shake for her. The bill came to $4.03 plus .20 tax and .40 tip,

Typical Expenses for a Four-Person Urban Family *

GROSS ANNUAL INCOME	$10,971	$15,905
EXPENSES		
FOOD	2,532 (23%)	3,198 (20%)
HOUSING	2,638 (24%)	3,980 (25%)
TRANSPORTATION	964	1,250
CLOTHING AND PERSONAL CARE	1,196	1,740
MEDICAL CARE	612	638
OTHER CONSUMPTION ITEMS recreation, travel, tobacco, alcohol, books, records, etc.	684	1,129
MISCELLANEOUS life insurance, charity, gifts, savings, job-related expenses	560	937
TAXES	1,785	3,033
income taxes	1,366	2,614
Social Security payment	419	419

Consumption items (first 6 items) totaled 79 percent and 75 percent of the total incomes. The higher the income, generally, the lower the percentage spent for food and housing. This table has been prepared from U.S. Department of Labor, Bureau of Labor Statistics, Division of Living Conditions Studies, based on living costs in autumn, 1971, the latest available at the time this book went to press.

* This family consists of a husband, employed full time, nonworking wife, boy, 13, girl, 8.

total $4.63. The at-home cost tallied this way: one pound lean ground beef, $1.00, three buns, .24, lettuce, tomato, .10, three slices cheese .20, frozen French fries, .22, portions of one quart milk, one pint ice cream, chocolate syrup for milkshakes, .60. For $2.36, she could make the meal at home, with larger meat patties at about one half the cost of eating out.

The main thing in food costs, one economist explained, is to know what you are paying for. If costs seem out of line, step back and evaluate where your food dollar goes. You may be able to cut costs and eat better by being a sharper shopper.

Fashion Dollars

"Just because you wear clothes doesn't mean that you know how to buy them," a consumer education teacher comments. What you spend for clothes is a personal matter, depending on your circumstances: what you do as a student, the climate where you live, how you spend your spare time, whether you work and where you work, your likes and dislikes, and the amount you can afford. Whatever your particular circumstances, you can do better by more knowledgeable, selective shopping. Here's how:

1. Impulse buying is out. Buy with a plan. Any plan is better than none at all. Shop for specific things. Cut off spur-of-the-moment buying of items you don't truly need. A bargain is worthless unless you really will use it. Jenny had too many bad buys hanging in the closet, so she decided to test every possible purchase by asking herself, "Do I absolutely have to have this right now? Can I live without it?" Surprisingly she got along very well without many things she would once have bought hastily as long as she had a charge plate in hand.

2. Buy good quality coats, shoes, sweaters—anything that you wear a lot.

3. Go through your closet and drawers at least twice a year. You may find something you had forgotten that will work well now.

4. Make an attempt to learn your own clothing tastes. You may think this knowledge is automatic, but it is not at all. Do you prefer mod, far-out things? Or does your taste run more to the tailored, conservative look? Or are you comfortable in very feminine clothes? What is your image of yourself?

5. Evaluate your clothing mistakes. What do you buy that ends up hanging in the closet, rarely worn? Are all your clothes "bombs" in the same area—dress-up things, pants, T-shirts, or whatever? Have you bought clothes that fit poorly and that you later disliked? Or have you bought things a friend or advertising influenced you to buy, though they were not really suitable for you? Discipline yourself not to repeat the same mistakes. Don't buy what fashion says is the in thing to wear if it is not becoming to you. Have you ever seen a chubby girl wearing a skinny-rib sweater, with a clingy, wide midriff?

6. When you find one maker/designer whose things fit you well, look for more of the same.

7. Don't overlook the dime store for T-shirts, faddy jewelry, scarves.

8. If you are handy, learn to sew some basic, easy-to-sew things, skirts, pull-on pants, tunic tops. Save your dollars to buy hard-to-sew items, such as shirts, jackets.

9. If you are small-to-medium build, try the girls' department rather than juniors or misses for jeans, shirts, sweaters, sportswear. You can find lower prices, good styles. Ann bought a ski jacket in the girls' department made by exactly the same maker in the identical down-filled fabric, for one third less than she would pay in women's wear.

10. Boys' and mens' departments are good places to find shirts, sweater vests. You'll find good color range and style at much lower prices than in women's departments.

11. Go shopping the Army-Navy circuit for basics such as jeans, outdoor wool shirts. You'll find quality at low prices.

12. Keep your wardrobe of separates to three basic colors, unless you're really fickle. One well-dressed teen buys everything to mix and match in two colors, each season, then uses accessories to extend her wardrobe.

13. In shoes, keep away from off-beat colors that are hard to work into a wardrobe. Stick to basics, such as brown, tan, black, white, navy, unless you find a great sale.

14. Read the labels in garments. If the suit is 100 percent polyester, but the trim is nonwashable, you'll probably need to have the item dry-cleaned unless you remove the trim each time. Dry-cleaning can add expense as well as inconvenience over the lifetime of a garment. If it has to be dry-cleaned, will you wear it less?

15. Last, but far from least, don't buy clothes to give yourself a lift when the world looks gloomy or the midwinter blues set in. Experiment with a new makeup or find another way to get out of the doldrums. Do something you never have done before—a craft, a hobby, a sport—but don't rush out on a clothes-buying binge to mend a broken heart.

Judging Quality in a Garment

The first time Suzy washed a twenty-dollar dress, a ten-inch section tore out in the hem and a side seam split in two places. The hem had only been basted in with large stitches. Suzy's experience is all too common. You can guard against the same thing happening to you by learning something about quality in clothing. Here's a checklist that should help:

1. Read the label carefully, so you'll know what the fabric is and what care it requires.

2. Always try things on to check for proper fit. Even blouses and sweaters may vary in fit from one maker to another. Sizes are not always an indication of fit.

3. Make sure seams are wide, at least one-half inch. They should be pressed open and lie flat. Edges should be overcast or should be pinked to avoid raveling. Cheap dresses may have as few as seven stitches to the inch on the seam, while good dresses have twelve to fifteen. Synthetic fibers particularly need generous seams with overcast edges, since these fibers ravel easily. If seams appear to pucker, ask the store to redo the seams or find another garment.

4. The hem should be at least two inches and should not show on the right side. If the dress must be dry-cleaned, the hem should be finished with binding.

5. Facings should be stitched so they won't show on the right side.

6. Stress points should be reinforced, with diagonal stitching at pocket corners for strength.

7. Buttonholes should be firmly stitched with no loose threads at ends. They should be smooth and reinforced at ends and should be properly lined up with buttons. Buttons, hooks, and snaps should be firmly attached and properly placed.

8. Zippers should be in good working condition and should lie flat and smooth. They should be well covered when closed. They should be the right color and weight for the garment. A heavy-weight garment should not have a lightweight, fine zipper.

9. Designs (checks, stripes, plaids) should match at seams.

10. If you buy pants that are 100 percent cotton, check the label carefully when you try them on. Are they preshrunk? Or must you buy a larger size to insure proper fit after they are washed?

11. If collar and trims are a contrasting color, they should be removable for washing.

12. A no-iron garment should not have packaging wrinkles or folds from the fabric maker. They may be permanent.

Evaluating a Major Purchase

One research study claims that teen-agers buy one half of all camera and photo supplies in the United States. How do you choose which shutter to click, which camera suits your shutterbug situation? Using a camera as the focus, learn how to go about shopping and evaluating any major purchase.

Rick wanted a camera and his requirements were simple. He wanted to take snapshots on vacation, for special events, and to record events and people. He planned to have a photo album in which he could look at his shots easily. Knowing his needs from the start helped narrow his requirements. Rick started by going to a specialty shop, the largest camera shop in town, where he knew the selection would be large and the clerks should know a lot about various cameras. He had no intention of buying his camera on this first shopping trip. He was shown several camera types and soon narrowed his choices to either a thirty-five millimeter or a pocket instamatic. He was told that the thirty-five millimeter would produce sharper prints and would suit his needs for a long time, even as a serious photographer. He was shown some superb black-and-white photos taken with a thirty-five millimeter camera, one of a weathered and wrinkled old man sitting by a shed and another of sprinklers in a wheat field at dawn, silhouetted in intricate patterns. Rick agreed that these photos were indeed impressive.

Rick also saw lovely snapshots, both color and black-and-white, taken with a pocket instamatic. The pocket cameras were less expensive, took cartridge-type film, and were simple to load and unload. He looked at three different brands, several models of each. Higher-priced instamatics could take slides, although thirty-five millimeter slides were recommended if slides were important to Rick. Rick would need a projector for slides, and he could not view his shots as easily as he could with a snapshot album. Rick decided that his present interest did not include slides. He compared features and prices on all models.

Rick's next stop was the library, where he checked the *Readers' Guide to Periodical Literature*, under cameras. He also checked *Consumer Guide* and *Consumer Reports Annuals*. He found several magazine articles on thirty-five-millimeter cameras, and two on "the new instamatics." In a photography magazine he read about the superior quality of photos he might be able to shoot with a thirty-five millimeter. In a consumer magazine, he found ratings of both thirty-five millimeter and pocket cameras. The pocket cameras were divided into low-priced cameras and high-priced ones. The high-priced ones were $100 and up, out of his price range. Comparative judgments were made by the magazine's experts, and features, shutter speeds, types, and speed of films were listed, as well as negative factors about each model. Rick decided the ease of handling an instamatic appealed to him, since he was a novice photographer. He narrowed his choice to two possible models, then checked out the consumer magazine to study them further at home.

Once he made his decision, he went to a department store and several discount stores to check the prices. He also checked two major mail-order catalogs. He recognized that the camera-shop price would probably be higher, for they had spent time with him, and this time cost would be figured into the pricing. He wondered if the discount house would be as good as the specialty shop should anything go wrong with his camera, even though it was a major brand. Since the price differential was not much, Rick decided on the camera shop.

In some cases, the price difference reflects things like gift wrapping, "free" delivery, and charge accounts rather than cash-and-carry, informed clerks rather than self-service, or maybe only a label in a coat that says you bought it at a posh store. Each of us must decide what things are important to us, and whether we need to extend our buying power. Whether you want to buy skis, a camera, tape recorders, or clothing, you could use the same evaluation process. Weigh the features each product has, then decide

When to Buy What

JANUARY

coats, cosmetics, dresses, drugs, furs, glassware, handbags, hosiery, lingerie, men's suits, shoes, sportswear.

FEBRUARY

bedding, china, housewares, men's shirts, sportswear, Washington's birthday specials.

MARCH

appliances, Easter specials, garden supplies, luggage, silver, spring specials, winter clearances.

APRIL

cleaning supplies, coats, dresses, fabric, hats, lingerie, paint.

MAY

air conditioners, carpets, Mother's Day specials, outdoor furniture, summer sportswear, tires, TV sets, white goods.

JUNE

bedding, camping gear and supplies, dresses, fabric, furniture, women's shoes.

JULY

air conditioners, handbags, housecoats, lingerie,
radios and stereos, sportswear, swimwear.

AUGUST

back-to-school specials, coats, furniture, furs,
garden equipment, summer clearances, white goods.

SEPTEMBER

auto accessories, cars, china, fabric, fall fashions,
home furnishings, men's and boys' wear, silver.

OCTOBER

carpets, Columbus Day and Veterans' Day specials,
fall and winter sportswear, major appliances, ski supplies,
snow tires, women's coats.

NOVEMBER

china, Christmas toys and gifts, coats,
Election Day and Thanksgiving Day specials,
linens, women's winter clothes.

DECEMBER

Christmas gifts, end-of-month reductions
on Christmas cards, wrappings, decorations,
men's suits, resort and cruise wear, used cars.

what features you are willing to pay for. Not only *where* you shop, but *when* you shop can make a difference in the price you pay.

If you shop for standard items in clothes, things like jeans, underwear, socks, or stockings, a discount house or large chain store may be your best bet. But if you want something special and more stylish, specialty shops are likely to have the best offerings. These stores have seasonal clearance sales, if you can wait and take the risk of finding what you want at that time. There are traditional sale times of the year for many items, from lingerie and linens to Christmas gift items and cards. The chart on pages 86-87 gives details on what to buy when.

—by a sparing use of ready money
and by paying scarcely anybody—
people can manage, for a time at least,
to make a great show with very little means.
WILLIAM MAKEPEACE THACKERAY

6

Make the Most of Your Money

Borrowing, saving, and spending money is an art. One consumer advocate says that the average middle-income family expects to handle between one half to three quarters of a million dollars during a lifetime of earning. Half a million dollars, that sounds like a lot of money. But how much of it will merely drift away? It all depends on how well one handles money. Experts say you can save up to 20 percent of the money you receive in a lifetime by being a supersharp consumer. Whatever you save, it can give you added pleasures in your life.

If you have money you don't need immediately, let that money earn more for you. Let it work as hard as possible to give you the best return. As with most things, you'll have to shop for the best place to put your money to work.

Where to Save

There are several possible places to deposit your hard-earned dollars, and a regular commercial bank is the most common. These banks pay the lowest interest rates, perhaps only 4 or 5 percent, and they are usually "full-service" banks, which means they offer safe-deposit boxes, checking accounts, and loan facilities. The maximum rate they can pay is determined by Federal law, and this rate goes up or down from time to time. Not all banks pay the maximum allowable rate.

Some commercial banks have devised special types of savings accounts or savings certificates, which carry higher rates (about 1½ percent higher than a regular account) if you leave your money in the account for a longer time, typically two years. If you withdraw before the agreed-upon time, you forfeit some or all of the bonus interest.

Savings banks pay slightly higher interest than commercial banks, but these banks don't exist in all states.

Savings-and-loan associations are generally allowed to pay a higher interest rate than other banks. They also offer time certificates for long-term savings. For example, you may invest $500 in a one-year certificate, in order to earn 6 percent interest. Some banks allow you to invest as little as $100 in such certificates, while others require that you invest at least $1000 to earn highest possible interest rates. Banks pay higher rates if they can rely on you to let them use your money.

Credit unions, another place where you can save money, are nonprofit organizations sponsored by certain industries, labor unions, fraternal organizations, or groups with some common bond. Their interest rates usually range higher than those paid by banks.

If your savings are intended for long-term use, perhaps for college, consider a time certificate. If you expect to need money in a short time or want to have easy access to it, then time deposits aren't for you. Some banks, however, do have a ninety-day, automatic-renewal certificate, which earns higher interest than a regular passbook account. This deposit plan may also suit your needs.

How is the interest on your account figured? The best way is the one used for the Day-of-Deposit to the Day-of-Withdrawal account, sometimes called DD-DW. In this case, no matter when you deposit your savings, they begin to earn interest until you withdraw them. Some "regular" savings accounts don't work this way, so be sure to ask. They may pay interest only if your money is in the account for the entire interest-paying period, often as long as three months. They may advertise "in by the tenth earns interest from the first"; but this inducement may also mean that anything deposited after the tenth of the month waits until the next month or even the next quarter before it begins to earn interest. Also, if you withdraw money before the end of an interest-crediting period, you may lose all the interest.

For example, Mark withdrew his entire $600 savings from the bank on June 20, when he moved to another part of the city where he planned to open a new account. The bank credited interest earnings on the last day of each quarter, so Mark lost $7.50 by withdrawing before June 30. Had he realized, he could easily have waited ten days.

If you move money in or out of a bank at the wrong time, you may lose money. Be sure to ask the bank how much you will save or lose before you make your deposit or withdrawal.

Interest paid to you is compounded daily, quarterly, or monthly. In actual money, though, which way makes little difference. If you had $1000 in a savings account for one year, it would earn you only twenty-five cents more if compounded daily than if compounded quarterly at the same interest rate. A very large sum of money over a long period of time would make a big difference.

Don't assume the bank statement you receive monthly or quarterly is always correct. Mike, seventeen, didn't bother to keep the receipts for the deposits he made when he had his first summer job. When he received his bank statement, the final balance looked surprisingly small to him. "I've been making deposits every week now for six weeks. I was sure I had a lot more in my account than this," he complained. He still had his paycheck stubs, so he checked them over carefully to see if he could recall cashing any of them without making a bank deposit. Mike figured that he had deposited between thirty and forty dollars each time. A phone call to the bank showed they actually had credited him with one deposit he could not account for, but had not recorded in his account two or three deposits he remembered making. He made a trip to the bank, armed with his paycheck stubs and his account book. Unfortunately, he had not recorded his deposits in his book, and he had no proof of deposit. "I didn't think I needed the receipts," he said. "I just assumed the bank didn't make such mistakes."

After nearly an hour's time spent with the bank clerk, the errors were discovered. Three of Mike's deposits had been credited to his brother's account. The account numbers were almost identical —except for one digit—and the clerk had not checked the name and number on the account carefully. In fact, several deposits had been made in name only, with no account number given, since Mike had made deposits without coded deposit slips bearing his account number. The deposit they had credited him for that was not his belonged to his brother.

Check your bank statements carefully, and keep a complete record of deposits and withdrawals.

Christmas Club accounts may encourage you to make a weekly deposit of a certain amount, but these accounts earn no interest in most states. If you made the same deposit in a regular account, you'd get a few dollars in interest at the end of the year.

United States Savings Bonds offer a way to earn interest on a small sum. You can invest as little as $18.75 for a $25 bond, but you must keep it to maturity to get the full interest. If you cash your bond in earlier, you get less interest. Young people may find bonds a convenient way to save, since you can often buy them through automatic payroll deductions. "If I don't see it, I don't spend it," explains Ellen, who has her first job as a typist.

The stock market has great appeal to a young person as his savings in a bank mount up. He knows that inflation (the rising cost of goods) eats away his interest if he invests in fixed-dollar savings, where he gets back what he puts in plus interest. He begins to consider buying stock, which is actually buying a part ownership in that business. In this way, the buyer hopes to protect himself against inflation. Sometimes the plan works well, but sometimes not. To begin with, the small investor pays more in commission to the broker who buys his shares for him than if he could buy a block, or 100 shares, at a time. You can buy shares only through a stockbroker. Your stock does pay dividends, usually more than you would get from a bank. Stock prices go up and down for many reasons, and they can be very low when you need your money. In fact, there's no guarantee that your stock will go up in value. Unless you can leave your money invested for quite a few years, and you don't need it for emergencies, you should stick to safer places.

Checking Accounts

Over fifty million of us have personal checking accounts, but not all of us take full advantage of them. As a young teen-ager, you probably do not want to have a checking account, since the few checks you write would not justify the charge banks make to carry your account. There are two basic types of checking accounts, the "special" and the "regular." A regular checking account usually requires you to have a certain minimum balance (perhaps $200), and you are then charged a fixed fee for each check you write, possibly .10. Your $200 draws no interest, and if your balance falls below that minimum, you are typically charged a $2.00 per month service charge. Some banks offer free checking if you keep a balance of $250 or $300 in your account at all times. A special checking account, where you are not required to have a minimum balance, will likely require a maintenance charge of $2.00 per month, plus .10 or .15 per check that you write. If you write only a few checks on that account, a special checking account is generally better for your needs. Either way checking accounts may cost you money. When you are ready to have a checking account, call a few banks to get checking account costs. You should also determine if the convenience of a neighborhood bank is important to you.

Susan, for example, opened her checking account in a bank across town because they were attracting new business by offering a no-charge checking account. Although she did most of her banking by mail, she too often found that she had to rush across town to get her deposit in or to get cash before the bank closed.

Most banks pay postage both ways for deposits and withdrawals; banking by mail may suit you if you can plan far enough ahead so you won't be caught short when you need to cover checks or get funds for a weekend trip.

Types of Credit

"It's so easy to buy and buy and buy, everything you think you need," a young couple told a debt-counseling service. "Then after a while you begin to think the whole thing will just swallow you. I can't sleep, I'm so uptight," seventeen-year-old Jennie confided. Depressed and near the brink of mental breakdown, this couple is not unique. In thousands of cases each year, mounting debts cause all kinds of grief, from ulcers to suicide attempts to divorce. Money problems are rated as one of the top concerns in marriage conflicts among people under thirty years old.

Convenient credit isn't cheap. If you put your leather coat on a charge account, the 1½ percent per month interest can wipe out your bargain. Your low-priced find becomes a high-priced luxury. Credit comes from banks, credit unions, finance companies, and retail stores. Some charge more than others. Do you know what you are paying for credit? Ask yourself, "Is having something *now* worth the added credit costs? Can I meet the payments and have something left for fun?"

Single-use credit cards, ones used in a specific store or establishment only, are a common type and are issued by department stores, motel chains, and gasoline companies. Bank credit cards are issued free, such as BankAmericard and Mastercharge, and they allow you to charge almost anywhere. But is the service really *free*? Establishments who honor these cards pay a service fee of 5 to 8 percent of the purchase to the credit-card company, and, of course, the charges are reflected in the pricing of their merchandise or services.

Chris argued, "I should use a credit card, since I pay the same price whether I charge it or not." True enough! But having the card may tempt you to buy more than you can pay for without having interest charges added on. Handing a check-out clerk the charge card somehow seems less painful than forking over hard cash. Impulse buying or spending comes more easily with a wallet full of credit cards. The interest charge stated as 1½ percent per month looks trivial at a glance. Yet it is 18 percent per year, the maximum rate allowed by law for merchandise bought, nearly four times what your savings account pays you. Establishments where charge cards are not honored will usually charge less, as you may learn by comparison shopping.

Another type of credit card is used for travel and entertainment, such as American Express or Diner's Club, for which you pay an annual membership fee of about fifteen dollars. No interest is charged if you pay within thirty days, after which you pay 1½ percent per month, 18 percent per year.

Sometimes there's no charge if you pay an account within thirty days. However, more than likely, a specific billing date is stated on your charge-account bill. Carefully note that it says, "Payment must reach this office by. . . ." Sometimes you get barely enough time to put your payment in return mail before 1½ percent of the previous month's balance is added as a carrying charge. Some stores are now initiating a new way to determine interest charges, a method called "average daily balance." Your finance charge is computed on the average daily balance on your account. For example, on June 1 your account debit was $200. On June 10, you paid $100. Therefore, for ten days of the billing period your balance was $200, and for twenty days it was $100. To figure your average daily balance, multiply ten (days) times $200, then multiply twenty (days) times $100, add both and divide by 30 (days in that month). In this case, your average daily balance was $133.33. You would, at 1½ percent per month, pay $2.00 in interest for this month, as opposed to only $1.50 interest if the interest was computed on your actual balance after the tenth of the month. Most stores have a minimum finance charge of at least .50 should any unpaid balance remain on your account. As you can see, charging more than you can pay for in one billing period is costly.

A furniture or appliance store may offer you an "installment account" if you make a major purchase. Jim bought a stereo for $500, to be paid for in twelve monthly payments. The store quoted the finance charge at 6.7 percent on the total amount, saying that it would be $33.50. In actual fact, this interest rate is slightly over 12 percent true annual interest, since Jim did not have the full use of the $500 for the entire year. The United States Department of Agriculture states this formula as one method of figuring the true interest rate when payments are made monthly:

$$R = \frac{24\ C}{B\ (n + 1)}$$

Where:

R = annual true interest rate
C = Total finance charges in $
B = amount of credit received
n = number of payments needed to discharge the debt

Using this formula, the approximate true annual interest in this case would be:

$$R = \frac{24 \times 33.50}{500 \times (12 + 1)} = \frac{804.00}{6500} = 0.1236 \text{ or } 12.4\%$$

Truth in Lending laws require creditors to state charges in a uniform way so the consumer can make a comparison. An installment contract or a charge-account billing must state the finance charge (the actual amount of money you pay for credit), any service charge, interest or carrying charge, plus the annual percentage rate. Both these figures must be displayed clearly and prominently on forms and statements. A verbal promise of no service charge is worthless. Be sure it is in writing on your sales contract.

Suppose you borrow $100 for a year and are charged $6 interest. If you use the entire $100 for one year and do not pay it back until the end of that year, you are paying an annual percentage rate of 6 percent. But if you pay it back in twelve equal monthly payments, you are not using the entire amount for the year. The $6 credit charge in this example becomes 11 percent annual interest. You can use the Department of Agriculture formula to determine the figure.

A consumer credit counseling service in New York City says that many Americans are "credaholics" who live in an unreal world. Like gamblers and alcoholics, they won't admit they have a problem and insist their difficulties are temporary. An estimated 80,000 of the New York City metropolitan population go to court each year because they are in credit trouble. If so, how many more must be in trouble of slightly less magnitude?

When Bob M. got married four years ago, he and his bride took out a $500 loan to help furnish their new apartment. Two children, nine credit cards, and five loans later, this young bank clerk owed over $6000, more than he earned in six months. At Christmastime, he was so far behind in his bills that he couldn't charge one thing more. Bob feels that he is a casualty of the "easy credit approach," with which banks and finance companies encouraged him to borrow far more than he could repay. "Even when I was bumping my credit ceiling, they never said 'no.' They just offered more."

Financial experts say that Bob, in his early twenties, is typical of Americans who are in debt trouble. As a rule of thumb, no more

than 20 percent of your take-home pay should be spent to meet debt payments. According to experts, prime candidates for becoming "credaholics" are "young couples who don't have good communications with each other and can't talk about money because money represents power."

Borrowing Money

We *are* encouraged to borrow money freely, and taking a fantastic vacation or buying an expensive bike without having to pay for it right away can be tempting. A California credit union actively seeks youth loans by sending out applications and offering quarterly newsletters. The application suggests that young members might need cash for phonograph records, travel, stereo equipment, bikes, or *any good purpose!*

You could borrow to "give vacation a whole new meaning for a youth tour of Japan or Europe." Or perhaps you only need a "bus ticket to see a friend who lives up the coast." At sixteen you may borrow up to $200 and take fifteen months to repay, at the rate of $14.43 per month. At thirteen you may borrow $50 for twelve months. In either case, you need only have some source of income, from family allowance to a paper route. A parent's consent is required, although they are not cosigners, and he or she is not responsible for the debt if you don't pay.

Although response to this loan program was not overwhelming, young people did borrow $5862 in the first year. Loan requests sometimes included a copy of the applicant's report card or a letter explaining how they would repay the loan. Loans were made for bicycles, Christmas gifts, school clothes, batteries, etc. The program was intended to help teach responsibility and good saving habits, according to the credit-union manager. She explained that the young people did pay their loans on time, and none became delinquent.

You can also borrow money on bank credit cards for a healthy charge. A "set-up" charge of 4 percent, with a maximum of $15, is made for a cash advance, in addition to the finance charge of 1 or 1½ percent per month (12 or 18 percent per year) on the balance you haven't paid twenty-five days after the closing date of your account. If you borrowed $200, you are then charged $8 for "set-up," even if you did repay in one billing period. In addition, if your payment reaches the office late, you are charged a late charge of $1.

Finance companies also loan money, usually at very high rates. Mike, sixteen, had an interesting experience while researching a consumer-education class project. He called five finance companies listed in the yellow pages of the phone book in his town and asked to borrow $500 for twelve months to buy a used car. He was usually told only what the monthly payments would be. After more probing, he found the total interest charge and finally, after repeated questions, the true annual interest rate was revealed—a shocking 30 to 36 percent. In fact, one company quoted its rate as 32 percent, when in truth it was over 35 percent. At this rate, you would pay about $125 interest to borrow $500 for one year.

Although on the phone Mike had a difficult time learning the true rate, on the loan contract the lender would be required by law to state it clearly. He would also have to spell out any penalty if you decided to pay off your loan. Dealer financing, when the seller offers to help you with the financing, is an expensive route to follow and could cost you up to 48 percent depending on your state laws. A bank or credit union usually charges less to borrow money than a loan company. Know what you are being asked to pay before you sign any such contract. Loaning money is big business. In fact, an official of Bank of America says bank credit cards are still the biggest money-makers the bank has out of all the various ways to use bank funds.

Many people somehow feel intimidated about going to a bank for a loan. They may think the color of their skin or whether they are fashionably dressed is important in getting a loan. Such considerations are not. As long as you are neat and presentable, you should not be concerned about your appearance when you apply for a bank loan. Banks are in business to lend money to make more money. You will be considered on the kind of credit risk you represent to the loan officer. He judges you on the three C's of consumer credit: Capacity to Repay, Capital Worth, and Credit Experience.

In your case, the capacity to repay will likely be most important. Do you have a part-time job or income from some source? Do you have other debts? You will be asked to fill out a loan application stating these things. Capital worth is concerned with your assets— such as car, motorcycle, house—the things you own that might cover the loan, if you can't repay it. Credit experience is your past record of paying bills on time. Just because you have never borrowed money before is no reason to think you will be refused a loan. When you apply for credit the first time, you are judged in other ways, including type of job, income, reason for borrowing the money, and possibly even your academic record, if you are a student.

You can also borrow from yourself, probably the cheapest way to borrow. This method requires that you have money in the bank, and then you can borrow against it. You pay interest, but your savings account continues to collect interest. The difference between these two interest rates is far less than taking a bank loan without savings. Your savings are held by the bank as collateral, and you cannot withdraw your funds until you have paid back the loan. This procedure may seem silly to you. Why not just withdraw your money? However, the passbook loan gives you added incentive to repay yourself and enables you to collect at least some interest for the loan period.

Credit Cards

Does a wallet full of credit cards make you an impulsive buyer? Try leaving them at home when you go shopping to see new merchandise. You may find that you compare price and quality more carefully. If you are forced to come back the next day to buy something, the cooling-off period may have dimmed your enthusiasm. Mary Ann, eighteen, a secretary, and a girl friend couldn't resist browsing through the shopping center almost every weekend. Shopping was something to do, and it was fun. In fact, suburban malls have a variety of entertainment from art shows to antique auto collections designed to attract browsers. In one fall shopping season, Mary Ann had picked up seventeen "sale" items, ten of which simply didn't work out. Among the buys were clunky jewelry, which she later despised, a brown knit halter, which she had nothing to wear with, a trench coat too similar to one that she already owned, and velvet pants, which fit poorly. All were nonreturnable sale items. Her credit-card bills began piling up.

The crowning blow came when Mary Ann received two bills for things she didn't buy, a camera for $80 and luggage for $130. She quickly checked her wallet and discovered that two cards were indeed missing. Would she have to pay for the purchases? By Federal law, you are protected against unauthorized use of your credit cards. If the card is lost or stolen, you are liable for a maximum of $50 in charges made by someone else. However, if you notify the card issuer before any such charges are made, you are not responsible for any amount. You are not responsible either for any unauthorized charges on a credit card if the card was sent to you without your request or permission. The issuer must also provide on the card a place for identification of the user, such as signature panel or photo. The issuer is further required to provide you with a form to use in notifying him of the loss or theft of the card.

Mary Ann decided to weed out her credit cards, and she destroyed all but two of them. She also decided to shop with these questions in mind. "Do I absolutely have to have it? Can I live without it?"

If your credit card is lost or stolen, immediately notify the issuer, by phone, if possible. On an evening or weekend, doing so is difficult, since no one mans these offices or banks then. Send a telegram, or, if you have phoned, send a follow-up letter. Remember, though, if you have lost a wallet full of credit cards (nine is the average carried by shoppers), you may be liable for at least $450 if you delay reporting the loss.

Credit advertising often emphasizes how easy borrowing is rather than the actual cost of it. Some charge accounts say, "What cash can't buy," or "Think of it as money." Credit can be helpful and of great convenience, if it doesn't cause you to spend unwisely or too freely.

Strong and content I travel the open road.
WALT WHITMAN

7

How to Buy Your Wheels

Sooner or later everyone focuses his attention on wheels as a way of getting from here to there. Whether you buy a ten-speed bicycle, a trail bike, a motorcycle, or a used car, you'll want to evaluate your needs and your budget. What are your transportation needs at this time? Do you plan to ride around town strictly for pleasure? Will you need wheels to get to a job? Or do you plan to do some cross-country touring? What are the upkeep costs for these wheels?

The Bicycle Bug

According to the Bicycle Institute of America, Americans buy more than ten million bicycles a year. Over fifteen thousand miles of bikeways have been built in the 1970's and another hundred thousand miles are planned.

Once the bicycle bug bites you, how do you decide which bike is for you? That choice depends on what you plan to do with your bike. The experts in this field suggest that for riding a short distance to school and an occasional long ride, a single-speed or a three-speed bike would fill your needs. If you plan to do serious, long-distance touring, you'll want a five- or ten-speed bike.

A single- or three-speed bike is sturdy and well equipped to handle the wear and tear of city traffic and streets. It will also handle heavy accessories. The three-speed works well in stop-and-go traffic, since the gears can be changed as needed. You can stop in one speed and start in another. The handlebars are in a raised position for faster braking.

The multispeed, or deraileur, bike is lightweight and good for distance travel. These bikes look quite uncomfortable with their dropped handlebars. Yet cyclists find the forward-leaning position easy to get used to and efficient to pedal in. This handlebar style allows for even weight distribution and balance, decreased wind resistance, and precision handling. It also helps the body soak up road shocks and enjoy a better ride.

A ten-speed bike's gears must be changed while the bike is in motion. For example, when you stop for a traffic light, you must either resume pedaling at a higher speed than might be comfortable and then change gears as you are moving, or else you must get off the bike and change gears while turning the pedal with your foot.

Here are some checkpoints that should help you to make your bike purchase a happy experience:

1. Buy only from a reputable dealer who backs up his product and pledge of service. Major mail-order houses do offer reasonable prices as well as parts and service. Bicycling experts, however, recommend that for the safest buy, you should go to a bicycle specialty shop where bikes are sold and serviced. When the retailer receives a shipment of bicycles, they require many small adjustments, including brakes, wheel alignment, saddle heights, etc. If such adjustments are

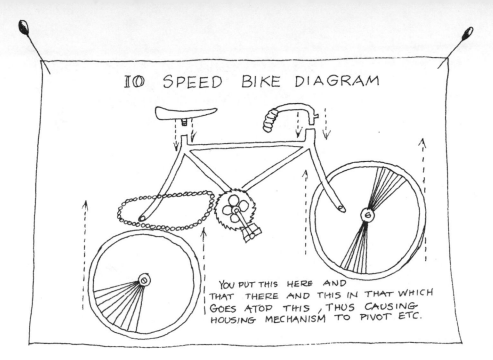

10 SPEED BIKE DIAGRAM

YOU PUT THIS HERE AND THAT THERE AND THIS IN THAT WHICH GOES ATOP THIS , THUS CAUSING HOUSING MECHANISM TO PIVOT ETC.

not properly made, the bicycle can be unsafe as well as hard to pedal.

Department and discount stores are not recommended for bicycle purchases. A poorly trained clerk may assemble your bike. The store may carry cheaply built bikes, and service is usually non-existent. Flashy paint jobs sometimes mask poor quality.

2. For a money saver, consider a used bike. If it's in top condition, expect to pay about 75 percent of the price of a new one. If the bike cost $150 new, you will pay about $100. If the bike is priced too low, consider whether it might have been stolen. Check for used-bicycle ads in the classified section of your newspaper. Inspect any used bike with great care. Ask to have a bicycle shop check it over before you buy.

3. Rent a bike and test ride it before you decide to buy. Check several models before you make this major investment. Never buy a bike you haven't ridden.

4. Lift the bike. The lighter the bike, the more it costs. A few pounds can make a tremendous difference in the way a bike responds. Many lower-priced ten-speeds weigh up to forty pounds. You should look for a bike that weighs from twenty-four to thirty pounds.

5. Check the frame joints. Look for a frame that is lugged (reinforced) at the joints, rather than one that has tubes stuck into each other and welded. A few major makes of ten-speeds have unlugged frames that are reinforced with extra brazing away from the stress joints. You can recognize this reinforcement by looking for a widening and an extra bead of metal at or near the joints. If a bike has reinforced joints, they help to make it more rigid. Even the strongest lightweight bike will flex under the strain of hard pedaling. Flexing from side to side and up and down may be almost unnoticed. But it means a lot of wasted energy for the rider who wants to go forward not sideways.

Men's frames with the bracing offered by the horizontal top bar are far more rigid than a standard women's model.

6. The brakes should meet the sides of the rims firmly when you press the levers no more than one inch. Both wheels should lock. Experts say that generally center-pull rather than side-pull brakes work best.

7. Wheel trueness, or proper adjustment, can be tested. With your finger on the brake block, spin the wheels to check for lateral (side-to-side) trueness. Ask the dealer to demonstrate for you that the wheels are not out of trueness more than 1/32 of an inch.

8. Check the bike parts carefully. Better bikes have aluminum rims, cranks, and hubs. Cheaper bikes have steel parts, and often they have one-piece steel cranks or steel-cottered cranks. The crank is the right-angled part to which pedals are connected.

9. Frame alignment can be checked by using a ruler to make sure wheels are centered between the fork blades and the rear-seat stays. Ride the bike with hands off the handlebars. Does the bike ride true and not pull to one side? You can also test the bike by walking it briskly around the showroom floor, holding the bike straight up by the saddle. If it shows a definite tendency to turn to one side, reject that bike. Such disalignment makes a bike very tiring to ride. Handlebars should not wiggle excessively, as they sometimes do when their support is not rigid enough. If you ride your bike on a wet street, the rear wheel should follow in the track of the front wheel if you are coasting straight. If it doesn't, the frame is not aligned properly.

10. Pedals should be slip resistant. Many bikes have serrated metal edges on the pedals, for better friction, rather than rubber or plastic treads. Ball bearings in pedals help the rider's pedaling action. Toe clips for pedals are valuable for long trips. They allow top efficiency, since you can pull up as well as push down. They are not recommended for city use, because you can't get your foot out of the pedal quickly.

11. Don't fall for ads that claim a bike has a racing-type kickstand. No racer would use any kind of a kickstand, since they are merely added weight. Bicycle expert Eugene Sloane considers kickstands "useless." Most better bicycles do not have kickstands. They allow a strong wind or passerby to knock the bike down.

12. Buy a bicycle that fits you. Straddle the top bar or tube with both feet flat on the ground. You should clear the top tube by one half to one inch. If you have less than one-half inch clearance, the bike is too big. You could be hurt if you make a quick stop or have to dismount quickly. For whatever price range or model you select, be sure you fit the machine to you. The seat and the handlebar should be at approximately the same level. The saddle height should be set so that your leg is almost fully extended, with a slight bend in the knee, when the ball of the foot rests on a pedal in its lowest position.

13. For defense against bicycle thieves, buy a top-quality chain and lock. The chain link should be at least three eighths of an inch thick. To lock up your bike, pull the chain through both the frame and the back wheel. Don't chain your bike to a parking meter. A thief can pull the chain right over the top. Cover the chain with old inner tubing to avoid scratching your bike. Register your bike with local police. This precaution will increase your chances of recovering your bike if it is stolen. You might also use a metal engraver to etch an identifying number on your bike.

14. To break in your bike seat, use a leather-softening material on the saddle. Vaseline or neat's-foot oil will do. Then pound the seat with a rolling pin or smooth stick. You won't be saddlesore after your first serious touring day if you do. But don't tackle a twenty-mile trip the first day. Work up to it gradually to give your body a chance to get into shape.

If touring by bicycle appeals to you, a good group to contact is the American Youth Hostels. They list and rate over one hundred bicycle tours around the country. They have also produced the North American Bicycle Atlas. Their address is: American Youth Hostels, National Headquarters, 20 West 17 Street, New York, N.Y. 10011. Local AYH councils often sponsor day-long and weekend trips.

Minibikes, Minicycles, and Motorcycles

A popular vehicle with children in recent years has been the mini-bike. Minibikes have a two-cycle, single-cylinder engine, lightweight tubular frame, and small (ten-inch) wheels. The engine is a lawn-mower engine converted to bike use. Many minibikes start with a pull-cord arrangement like a lawnmower. The small tires make such bikes unstable, and the steering ability is decreased by the square-cross-section tires. Many cheaper bikes have only rudimentary friction brakes. Brakes should be either disc or the internal expanding type found on cars. These bikes are considered by some product-testing services to have many safety hazards. The hot exhaust pipe on minibikes often protrudes too close to the rider's leg, which could cause a burn. Brake pedals are sometimes operated with the left heel, which is awkward for right-dominated children. Minibikes are all so low that if they are used on a street, an auto driver may not see the minibike until it is too late. These bikes are not intended for highway use.

If getting away from it all is your thing, the wheels you buy may well be on a motorcycle. Described by one cyclist as "one of the few freedoms left," motorcycling is finding a new image in our society. A major reason for the recent mushrooming motorcycle business is the highly individualized nature of cycling; the rider is by himself. The open road calls. You feel power under your hands to go at any pace you choose, within the limits of your cycle.

Cycle champion Brad Lackey is an authority on all types of off-road motorcycles. He considers durability and reliability as the two key factors for anyone interested in buying an off-road machine. "The middle of a desert or forest is no place for a machine to break down, and the urge to get away from it all can lead to some very lonely places."

There are three basic types of off-road machines: the minicycle, or trail bike; the enduro, or street-legal, off-road machine; and the desert racer.

The minicycle, or trail bike, can be a street-legal machine, but primarily has the ability to carry riders off the road. They are a favorite of sportsmen, since they are lightweight and easily transportable in campers or cars. "Minis usually have about five horsepower and relatively low gearing for climbing. They are a good starting machine for off-road riders, but they do have limitations. They lack real power for true trailblazing," Lackey explains.

Minicycles have larger wheels than minibikes, usually from ten- to sixteen-inch wheels. They also have heavy-duty shock absorbers, kick starters rather than a rewind pull starter, plus an engine designed for motorcycles. They have the advantage of being more compact than a full-size motorcycle. The larger the wheels and tires, the more stable the machine will be. It will be less likely to get knocked off course by road bumps and irregularities. If you plan to ride trails mainly, then you should buy a cycle that is specially designed for that purpose. The knobby tires with bold, blocky tread pattern used for off-road machines won't corner well on paved roads. They also function poorly on wet streets.

"The most popular off-road machine is the enduro type," Lackey explains. "Enduro is a term that describes a motorcycle suitable for both street and off-road use. Most enduros are in the 90-450 cc class, although the 175-250 cc machines are the most popular." Some distinguishing features of the enduro type are high fenders, knobby tires if used for off-road terrain, and exhaust pipes placed high on the cycle to give more ground clearance. Some experts believe this class offers the most value for the dollar. Enduros serve equally well for town errands or for a day in the country.

According to Brad Lackey, the enduro machine is a good off-road motorcycle to start with. The basic things to look for are features that insure trouble-free operation and rugged construction. He feels the 175 cc enduro is a proper beginning model for most teen-agers. A typical 175 cc enduro puts out 16.5 horsepower. Many of the best machines in this class are two-stroke, single-cylinder models. Some of the important features are: automatic oil injection, electronic ignition systems, rugged frames, adjustable shock absorbers, and front forks.

Adjustable front forks and rear shocks give the rider the ability to tune the machine to his exact weight and riding style. Front and rear brake-wear indicators are also major points to look for. Fuel tanks should have screw-on or rear-hinged caps that are flush with the fuel tank, rather than ones that hinge and open upward or forward. The handlebars should not be raised high. This position is too tiring and makes the cycle hard to handle.

The most readily identifiable feature of the trail bike, whether a minicycle or an enduro, is the upswept pipe. This design prevents the engine's being drowned when you ford a stream. A good exhaust has spark arresters on the muffler to minimize the danger of starting fires in dry country, forest, or grassland. Whatever sparks escape through these high-rise pipes burn out before they reach the ground. Trail bikes use the knobby tires, deep-cleated for good grip on dirt, weeds, or pine needles. Such tires skid dangerously on wet roads and wear out quickly compared to conventional street tires.

Many trail bikes are equipped with huge rear sprockets. Bigger rear sprockets make the bike slower, but give better ability to climb hills or ride along rough trails.

A bike intended for trail use should have good ground clearance to keep from being damaged by boulders or logs. Even with adequate clearance, a trail bike needs a steel guard plate to protect the engine from these obstacles. Some motorcycle experts feel that complete reliability is an aim, not a fact. For this reason, most trail biking is done on the buddy system. If one bike breaks down, you can still get back to civilization on the other.

The best way to find the motorcycle to suit your needs is to test ride various brands in the same price and power class. Each has a different "feel," and one will likely be more comfortable for an individual rider. If you stick to the major manufacturers, service, parts, and warranties should be no problem. Small outlets may be risky, both for after-sale service and for parts you may need.

Buy a good quality helmet, one with a label certifying that it is approved by the Snell Memorial Foundation. This foundation has high safety standards for impact and resistance to penetration. One cyclist placed his new helmet on his motorcycle seat while he put his jacket on. The helmet rolled off, hit the pavement, and shattered. You can minimize your risks by always using protective equipment when you ride a motorcycle.

Buying a Used Car

In spite of all the pitfalls, many teens are learning to use their money wisely. Mark, seventeen, tells how he bought a used car. As part of a consumer-education class at Hanford High School in Richland, Washington, Mark tackled the job of evaluating how to buy a car to suit his needs and budget. He began by getting information from the library, where pamphlets on loan information and on used-car facts were filed. Then he visited more than a dozen car lots. "I had to consider what I could pay and what I needed in a car at this time," Mark explained, "so that helped pin it down somewhat."

"Most of the salesmen were quite helpful," Mark commented. "I looked the car over from the outside for touched-up places, bad rust spots, for anything that might suggest an accident. I checked the tires to see if I'd need new ones."

Mark also learned to check doors, windows, to try all the buttons, lights, windshield wipers, and turn signals to be sure they worked properly. He looked for lubrication stickers to see if the owner had serviced the car regularly. Here are some of the other checkpoints Mark learned for his own purchase and for his class:

1. Shock absorbers. Rock the car by pushing down hard at each corner. The car should not continue to bounce after you let go. If it does, the shocks are worn.

2. Brakes. Press down hard on the brake and keep your foot on it for twenty seconds. The brake should not sink after initial pressure. If it does, you may have a brake-fluid leak. Check the brakes on your road test by making a series of abrupt stops. Brakes should feel solid under pressure.

3. Mileage. It is illegal to turn back the odometer, so you would assume the mileage is accurate. The only time the odometer may be changed is when the entire instrument panel has been replaced because of accident, and then the fact must be so stated at the time of sale. Average yearly mileage is about 12,000. If a car has been driven about 60,000 miles, it will soon need major repairs.

4. Transmission. Test drive the car. When you start the car it should catch smoothly, with either manual or automatic transmission. It should shift into other gears smoothly. If the car jerks or makes knocking or groaning noises, have a mechanic check the trouble before you buy. Transmission leaks should also be checked.

5. Compression tests. Mark took his car to a mechanic friend for a compression test on the engine. Uneven compression may show the need for a valve job or a complete overhaul.

6. Radiator and cooling system. Check under the car for any water leakage. Take off the radiator cap to see that water is clean and rust free.

7. Piston rings. After driving at about fifty miles per hour, slow down gradually to about fifteen miles per hour, then accelerate. If you see blue smoke, the car may need new piston rings.

8. Call a bank and ask the loan officer for information on the National Auto Dealer Association Used Car blue book.

Here are some other facts Mark uncovered: The best buy in a used car would probably be a two- to three-year-old model, which should cost 50 to 60 percent of the new value. Although such a car should still have a lot of usable life remaining, buying any used car can be risky. After you've checked what you can by yourself, find a diagnostic center to evaluate the car's condition professionally. For about twenty dollars, such centers will use their laboratory full of electronic equipment to tell you what the car's condition is. They will check the compression, the engine, front-end alignment, transmission, steering, and brakes. If at first glance you can't seem to find a diagnostic center in your town, try a little harder. Sears, Penney, and major tire companies may operate one near you. Armed with a professional report on the car, you now have more leverage to ask for a price reduction. Never pay the first asking price, and a good rule to follow is to expect 5 to 10 percent reduction.

Mark also learned that the words *guaranteed used cars* mean absolutely nothing. The claim must say what is guaranteed and for how long. Don't believe that a spelled-out warranty isn't needed. You should try to get a 100 percent guarantee to cover both parts and labor for a stated period of time, at least thirty days, possibly ninety. Sometimes a guarantee will specify that you and the dealer split repair costs. Be sure you have in writing what your guarantee covers and whether you are obligated to have work done by the dealer's garage.

Some automotive experts recommend that you buy a used car from a new-car dealer's lot, since this dealer gets trade-ins and probably better quality cars than a lot that handles only used cars. A new-car dealer also has his own service department, where he can make repairs on used cars. New-car dealers usually give a written guarantee on each used car. Ask for the name and address of the previous owner. In many states, the law says that you have a right to this information.

Since you assume some risk when you buy any used car, evaluate carefully *before* you sign an agreement. Make the salesman talk in terms of total price, not dollars per month. Be sure his stated total price agrees with the price he writes in on the sales contract. If a salesman begins to apply uncomfortable sales pressure, bow out quickly. Be wary of "system sales techniques," where a series of salesmen pressure you. Your original salesman may first convince you that indeed this car is for you. He may say, "I'll see if I can get the boss to agree to this price." Then a closing manager appears on the scene to tell you he can't possibly sell the car at this price, that he'd be losing money on it if he did. Such a system is designed to fatigue and confuse you, to get you to agree to terms you would not otherwise find acceptable. Any deposit you make may be forfeited if you change your mind. Don't sign a contract unless you intend to buy the car.

Economy Driving

According to American Motors professional driver Les Viland, all drivers can increase their mileage per gallon of gasoline if they work at it a little. Viland drove from New York to Los Angeles, a 3,300 mile trek, at speeds ranging from forty-seven miles per hour to a top speed of sixty miles per hour. In his Gremlin, he averaged 26.5 miles per gallon! He offers these suggestions for more economical driving:

1. Determine to drive in a manner that saves fuel. Attitude is an important element in economy driving.
2. Maintain a constant pressure on the accelerator. Smooth, steady speeds are ideal for economy; excessive speed wastes gas. At sixty miles per hour, approximately 11 percent more fuel is used than at fifty miles per hour.
3. Avoid jackrabbit starts. A car uses more fuel to build up speed and momentum.
4. Study traffic conditions ahead to avoid unnecessary stops; losing vehicle momentum means more gasoline will be used in regaining it.

Good drivers avoid braking by adjusting the car speed to traffic flow.

5. Turn off the engine when stopping for more than a minute; idling requires a rich fuel mixture. Even a minute takes more gasoline than is used in restarting. Racing the engine while the car is stopped will also decrease gas mileage.

6. Accelerate gradually while going uphill; at altitudes of 5,000 feet or higher, have the carburetor adjusted for a leaner mixture to conserve fuel.

7. Check tire pressure frequently. Underinflation increases the rolling resistance of the car and may have a marked effect on fuel usage. Inflate tires according to recommendations in your car-owner's manual.

8. Stay alert, exercise good judgment in varying traffic situations, and keep your car properly maintained.

Ignorance of the law excuses no man.
JOHN SELDEN

8

It's the Law

Do you sometimes feel that there are laws, rules, and restrictions everywhere you turn? Would you prefer not to have so many regulations? Would you like to be free to do anything you want? You could go to school only when you felt like it; you could drive a car before you were sixteen. Would you like to live where everyone did whatever they wanted to?

If you were a hermit and lived in a cave, you could get along pretty well without laws. But as soon as you put two people together, they will surely disagree on something. How would you settle these disagreements? You could fight it out, or you could discuss the matter by determining the facts. But facts appear differently to each person involved. A third party, someone not concerned personally, is often needed to listen to both sides to help settle the dispute. At that point laws enter the picture. People make laws for the good of everyone.

You are protected by laws from the time of birth (and even before) in many ways. Long before you can vote you are protected by the Constitution of the United States and its amendments, particularly by the Bill of Rights. As you take your first steps into the adult world, you run into many laws designed to promote safety, health, and protection of personal property. This chapter will look at some legal problems that commonly touch the lives of young people.

Most young people don't get into trouble with the law. Yet, according to the Federal Bureau of Investigation, young people under nineteen are charged with nearly half of all serious crimes in the United States. Youths account for the majority of all arrests for vandalism, arson, auto theft, larceny, and burglary. About 5 percent of our young people commit 50 percent of all crimes in our country, and over 1,000,000 young people are brought before juvenile courts each year. Many of these youths have done things for which no adult could be arrested. Young people come into the courtroom for creating a nuisance, loitering, running away from home, skipping school, or for being incorrigible. Some come into the judicial system because they have no adult to take care of them.

A young person's first brush with the law usually comes with the police. It may first involve breaking rules rather than laws. What's the difference between rules and laws? Laws are made by civil authorities and enforced by police and the courts. Rules are made by schools, communities, institutions, and they apply to things like dress codes, smoking, and park hours. You can get into trouble with the institution that made the rules, but they can't take you to court or charge you with a crime for breaking that rule. However, if you constantly break rules at school or in the community, then you may be charged with "being in need of supervision," or with being "chronically disruptive."

Arrests by Age

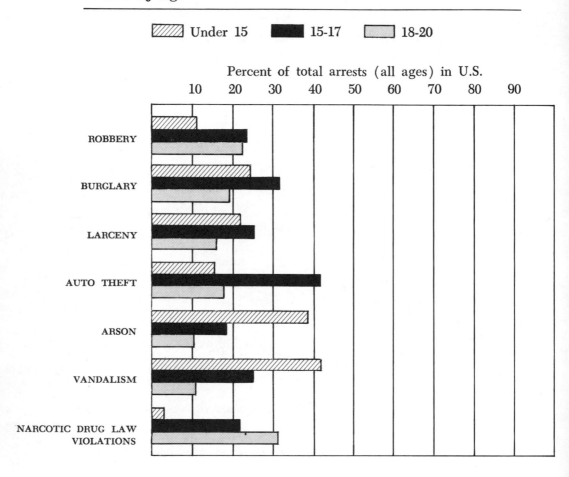

Compiled from Federal Bureau of Investigation,
Uniform Crime Reports, 1973

DEFINITION OF TERMS:

ROBBERY: Use of force or threat of force
to take something in presence of victim
BURGLARY: Unlawful entry to commit theft
LARCENY: Theft ($50 or more) without use of force

Legal Rights of a Minor

Often young people suffer a great deal of grief caused by lack of knowledge of the law. For example, David was having a party and his parents had gone out for a while. Music blared, and while most of the kids were dancing, a few had scattered through the house. Some played pool in a downstairs recreation room, and some were in David's room on the second floor. When police knocked at the door in response to a neighbor's complaint, David apologized and said they'd turn the music down lower. Officers asked to inspect the premises for possible drug use. David thought he had no choice, so he allowed them to come in. They found guests in an upstairs bedroom were smoking pot. Everyone at the party was charged with juvenile delinquency, possession of illegal drugs. David did not know that he didn't have to let the police enter the house without a search warrant. Police may enter by consent, or if an officer sees drinking or evidence of drugs, he may legally enter without a warrant.

In a Midwestern town ten young people picketed local grocery stores that refused to hire girls on an equal basis with boys for stock clerks and carry-out help. A police car arrived, and officers informed them they were breaking local laws that said, "Parading without a permit is prohibited." The young people indignantly replied, "This is our Constitutional right, since we are picketing peacefully." They stood their ground and refused to leave. As the officers arrested the group, two girls and two boys went limp and had to be carried into the police van. They were charged with juvenile delinquency: parading without a permit, creating a public nuisance, and resisting arrest. Going limp so you have to be carried or dragged by police has been interpreted as "resisting arrest."

If these young people had known more about the law, they would

not have protested police orders. They should have gone along quietly, then called their parents and a lawyer as soon as they arrived at the police station. Even though those involved in this case were cleared of parading without a permit, the charge of resisting arrest held up in court. These teen-agers actually had no intention of getting involved in a confrontation with the law, nor did they intend to be involved in violence.

Many of us have wrong ideas about the law as it applies to youth. Among these inaccurate ideas are:

1. I'm a juvenile, so nothing serious can happen.

2. If I'm innocent, I don't actually need a lawyer.

3. If I have a record as a juvenile, those records are closed so no one will ever know that I've been in trouble.

Each of these assumptions is completely false. In fact, the law is often more strictly applied to young people than to adults. A security officer from a department store told this story: A well-dressed matron dropped a bottle of Chanel No. 5 into her tote bag and headed toward the door. Not wanting to incur a potential customer's wrath, the store manager had the officer follow her and ask that she return the merchandise. Yet when a fifteen-year-old girl slipped a bikini under her baggy sweat shirt, the same store manager insisted upon calling the police "just to teach her a lesson." Since shoplifters steal three billion dollars in merchandise each year, many stores no longer look the other way when *anyone* steals.

Jim, sixteen, browsed in the record department of a large discount store. When he found the one he wanted, he absentmindedly put it on top of his notebook. Then he remembered something else he needed from sporting goods, and he decided that he would pay for both items at a central cashier. As he walked through the store, a detective stopped him. "I believe you have something that doesn't belong to you." Stunned, Jim tried to explain that he had several things to buy and that he planned to pay for the record at the check-out stand in sporting goods. Unfortunately for Jim, that check-out stand was moved a month ago.

Jim went along to the police station and tried to explain the facts. By the time his parents arrived, Jim had contradicted himself and seemed confused. A police officer suggested that he didn't need a lawyer, because after all he had the record in hand, poorly concealed by carrying it on top of a large notebook, and the verdict would be a simple matter. Jim protested, "I'm innocent. Don't you believe me? Why do I need to spend money to pay a lawyer when I haven't done anything?" Jim's father knew that Jim had intended to buy both a record and some tennis balls that day and that he had money from his paper route to pay for both. He also knew that the store had recently rearranged check-out stands. He felt sure that Jim was innocent, so a lawyer was hired.

Jim's case was dismissed when all the evidence was considered, but Jim learned a valuable lesson: Anyone formally accused of a crime, whether he is innocent or guilty, should have a lawyer to defend him. Recently the United States Supreme Court ruled that any accused person who cannot afford legal counsel shall be granted it free if the possible conviction could send him to jail for even one day.

When Brian applied for a summer job with a nuclear-reactor firm, he was asked, "Have you ever been arrested?" Brian once let a friend stash marijuana in the glove compartment of his car. Both boys were charged with possession of illegal drugs. Brian felt trapped. He had been found not guilty, yet he was arrested. Some judges feel that such questions should be illegal and that arrest records of juveniles should be erased. Some of these records have a way of haunting you. While an arrest doesn't mean a conviction, it can jeopardize employment or college admissions. In some states an attorney can petition to have a record erased. If erased, then a juvenile may legitimately answer "no" if he is questioned about his record in later life. Juvenile court records cannot be inspected without a court order. A juvenile offense may not keep a person from holding office or cause him to be denied application for a license. A delinquency finding is not a criminal conviction.

Susan, a recent college graduate, was denied a teaching job because, when she was nineteen, she had been arrested at a party where drugs were used. The applicant without an arrest record has a distinct edge over someone who has been accused of violating the law.

You should know that if you participate in a crime or profit from illegal gains in any way, you also share responsibility for this crime. When Brian allowed his friend to store drugs in his car, he was also charged with possession of illegal drugs. If you take a ride in a stolen car or if you buy bicycle parts from a stolen bike, you are considered an accessory to the theft. If you know that alcohol will flow freely at a party, stay away. Both drinkers and nondrinkers may be arrested. Illegal drinking accounts for almost as many arrests as for smoking marijuana.

Many law-enforcement authorities call our system a "revolving door." They mean that many youths come before the courts again and again, then later become adult criminals. One incredible statistic in the crime profile of our country is that 80 percent, or four out of five, of all people convicted of felonies (serious crimes, punishable by imprisonment) were at some earlier time convicted of some other crime. This first crime may have been a misdemeanor (a minor crime, punishable by fine or jail sentence) and has almost always happened while the offender was a juvenile.

Many cases that come into the courts each year involve property rights and negligence. While we are taught to respect property rights of others, we should also know our own property rights according to the law. If you kick a football through a neighbor's window, must your parents pay for it? They are legally *liable* (responsible) if you can be proven to be negligent, guilty of careless behavior. Your intentions don't count. The key question for such situations is: Were you acting as carefully as any reasonable person could be expected to? Few laws are black and white, and many times a lawyer will answer a question by saying, "It all depends." There are countless exceptions to most laws.

If you are a delivery boy or girl, you have the right to expect the property you walk on to be safe. If you are invited to come to someone's house and a defective porch step causes you to break your ankle, the owner is responsible for your medical care. Likewise, if you leave your baseball bat on the stairs in your house and a repairman is injured because of it, your parents are liable. You were careless or negligent. The property owner has the duty to maintain safe property. You may be considered guilty of gross negligence if you ride your bike through a crowded schoolyard. You would be considered in reckless disregard for the safety of others.

If a boy beats up your little brother and knocks out his teeth, or a gang smashes up your trail bike, must the parents of the offenders pay? Willfully injuring another person or his property is a crime. In both cases, the parents, who are liable until the offenders reach eighteen or twenty-one, must pay the damages. However, if the boy can prove that your little brother started the fight and that he hit him in self-defense, he may not be responsible.

You are home alone and a stranger comes into your yard and tries to attack you. Can you shoot him? The law says that you should retreat and that you may shoot only if you expect fatal injury or serious harm. You cannot claim self-defense if the force against you is a policeman trying to arrest you or a teacher trying to take you to the school office.

Suppose you blast your stereo, and a neighbor complains to the police. Can you be arrested for disturbing the peace even if your windows are closed? The answer depends on the time of the day and whether the noise was "substantial interference." Your neighbor has the right to enjoy her property quietly, just as you have the right not to be kept awake by her barking dog. Intent is not usually a consideration in a disturbing-the-peace charge.

What happens if you decide to skip school for a week? Each state makes laws about compulsory attendance at school, and most states require attendance between ages seven and sixteen or six through eighteen. Truancy is not a crime. But a habitual truant may be found delinquent and ordered to a special institution for juveniles.

Mike found a wallet containing $120 in a phone booth one morning when he stopped to rest after jogging. Jenny found an envelope of money in a parking lot. May either Jenny or Mike keep the money? The law of finders deals with both situations. Jenny and Mike have the right to their find against anyone *except* the true owners. Mike would likely be able to contact the owner by means of cards or identification in the wallet. He is obligated to do so and may be found guilty of larceny if he decides to keep the property when the owner is known. In most states Jenny must legally report her find and may be required to deposit it with the police for a period of time. If the owner doesn't claim the envelope, then it belongs to Jenny. Some laws say you must advertise or give public notice of found material.

In a large department store, Mark picked up a jackknife, looked it over for a while, then put it down. He handled several other items and looked around for his brother, who was to meet him there; then he walked away toward another department. The store manager stopped Mark and began to question him. Did the storekeeper have the right to quiz Mark? Many states have passed special shoplifting laws because of the magnitude of the problem. Since one in every fifteen persons who enters a store steals something, such laws may be well founded. In fact, the tennis racket you buy costs an additional 15 percent to cover the cost of shoplifted goods. These special laws say that a shopkeeper may question someone if he has reasonable grounds for suspicion. The shopkeeper cannot be sued for false arrest or malicious prosecution. "Shopkeeper's privilege" protects him. If you conceal on your person something offered for sale, so doing is prima facie evidence that you intended to steal it. The storekeeper would not have to prove intent, but rather you would have to prove you did *not* intend to steal it.

While some laws may appear to protect others, such as shopkeepers, other laws are made to protect everyone's freedom of speech—and freedom of press—even for things that shock or outrage others. In other words, if you shout down a speaker at a public meeting, or if you picket an auditorium to keep out an unpopular speaker, you infringe on the right to free speech and free assembly. Speakers may present their views, unless they are urging violence or inciting to riot, no matter how controversial these views are. All good ideas are not popular when they are first presented in society. Yet all viewpoints should be freely allowed. The press also has the right to print unpopular views, without fear of government censorship.

In a college newspaper case, Dickey v. Alabama State Board of Education, a student editor was ordered reinstated by a Federal

court after he had been expelled for deliberately breaking censorship rules. Gary Dickey wrote an article criticizing certain state legislators who tried to punish colleges if they allowed controversial speakers on campus. Dickey's faculty advisor vetoed the story, since a college rule said that editorials could not criticize the governor or state legislature. They could praise, but not criticize. The court, however, said that school officials couldn't infringe on students' rights or free expression as long as that right didn't "materially and substantially interfere with requirements of appropriate discipline in the operation of the school." The court decided that the censorship rule had nothing to do with maintaining order and discipline.

When You Break the Law

What happens when a juvenile breaks the law? In a typical case the youth is picked up and taken to the police station for questioning. Because personal freedom is highly valued in the United States, procedures for arrest and trial are carefully spelled out. When anyone, youth or adult, is brought into a police station, the law says that he must be advised why he is being detained. Then he must be advised of his constitutional rights. A juvenile has exactly the same rights as an adult—that is, the right to remain silent and the right to consult a lawyer or to have a lawyer appointed for him, if he cannot afford to hire one. He must be told that anything he says can be used against him in court, either in juvenile or adult court. If the police question a suspect without advising him of his legal rights, they act illegally. A confession of a juvenile is not admissable evidence if he has not been advised of his rights. A suspect is usually told his rights verbally, then asked to read and sign a statement affirming that he has been so advised.

After a juvenile is advised of these rights, his parents are called and his previous record is checked. Then police decide whether to release him to his parents, refer him to a social agency for counseling, or send him to juvenile court. While in criminal courts you are entitled to a jury trial, juvenile courts rarely follow this procedure. In juvenile courts, the trial is called a "hearing." The first hearing, or adjudicatory hearing, judges the act or situation. It is held as quickly as possible after the suspect is taken into custody. Sometimes no formal judgment is made, and a case may be continued while the judge, parents, and the court try to help the youth. After the first hearing, when all the facts are known and if the suspect actually committed the offense or needs supervision, a disposition hearing takes place. At this time the judge decides what should be done with the case. The youth may be released to parental custody, referred to counseling, placed on probation, or sent to an institution. The purpose of juvenile courts, even though they operate in a variety of ways from state to state, is to rehabilitate not to punish. They hope to help young people become useful, law-abiding citizens. The juvenile system handles youths under a certain age, which may also vary in each state. In most states, under eighteen is considered a juvenile, although this age may vary from sixteen to twenty-one.

Some juvenile cases are sent to adult court, since a juvenile court would have jurisdiction over a youth only until he reached twenty-one. If a seventeen-year-old commits a serious crime, such as first-degree murder, this case may then be handed over to adult court to insure control over the offender beyond his twenty-first birthday. Many traffic cases, including speeding and drunken driving, are automatically remanded (ordered back) to adult court in some states.

Sales Contracts

Hundreds of laws exist concerning sales, and many of them are stated in a document called the Uniform Commercial Code. If you are a minor, you may void almost any contract you make. This law protects the young from unwise agreements. Due to lack of experience, young people allow others to cheat them. Suppose you bought a minibike from a friend for sixty-five dollars, and when you brought it home, it wouldn't run. Are you simply stuck with a bad buy? No. Laws relating to contracts, sales, and their special application to youth would save the day. When you bought the minibike, you entered into a sale, which is a form of contract—one person promises to do something in consideration of something from another. You may ask the friend to give your money back, or you may sue him for it.

If your friend, a minor, sold you a camera, he could change his mind and demand his camera back, saying the price was not suitable to him.

A minor must disavow a contract within a reasonable time, and he may void a contract for any or no reason. If the minor has been emancipated, that is, no longer under his parents' guidance or has married, he is considered an adult for contract purposes. If you misrepresent your age and claim you are an adult, a contract is usually binding. If the contract is for "necessaries," such as food, clothing, or shelter, however, a minor must stick to the contract. The law is on your side when it comes to contracts with adults. An adult must honor a contract with a minor. The law protects you not the adult.

Just because you can get out of a contract for little or no reason doesn't mean that you should be careless about entering into one. Since buying habits developed as a teen-ager often continue throughout life, you should be well informed about anything you sign. Never sign a contract in which all the blank spaces are not filled in, and never sign a contract that you don't completely understand or haven't read. If something isn't clear to you, ask to have it explained. A bank-loan officer told about the typical borrower. "They are so anxious to have the loan approved that more than half of those who come to us to borrow never even read the contract! They just want to sign that piece of paper and get the money as fast as possible."

If an eighteen-year-old is considered an adult in your state, then when you reach eighteen, a contract will be binding for you. In some states you are considered an adult when you are legally married, no matter what your age. The law requires that you receive a copy of any contract you sign. Put it in a safe place for future reference.

Nineteen-year-old Steve bought a snazzy-looking used Porsche. He paid cash. The salesman assured Steve that he, himself, was a mechanic and could vouch for the good condition of the car. When Steve got home, he found a few words had been added to the sales agreement *after* he had signed it. "Speedometer turned back at 50,000 miles" made him question the salesman's reliability. After further checking at a reliable garage, he found the car had been welded, a good indication that it had been wrecked. Steve's father threatened to sue the dealer. This kind of publicity the dealer didn't need, so Steve got his money back. But most young people are not so lucky when they buy a used car and get stuck with a lemon.

If you sign a contract in a place other than the normal place of business, you may void that contract up to seventy-two hours afterward. For example, you sign a contract to buy silverware from a salesman who has given a demonstration party at a friend's home or in your home. You may change your mind and void the contract by sending a registered letter to the salesman at his home office. The letter must be postmarked within seventy-two hours after you signed the contract. This protection applies to both minors and adults.

Guarantees, Warranties

A guarantee is a guarantee, and it protects you when you buy a product. Right? Wrong! If a product is advertised as "guaranteed," that term can mean many different things. Mary Ann bought a major-brand electric typewriter that was "guaranteed for five years" as the warranty card boasted in bold letters. She read on. Down in the fine print she found that the guarantee for five years applied to parts only and that the machine had to be sent to a factory-authorized service center should it need repairs. Service centers were listed on the warranty card, and the nearest one to her home was two hundred miles away. She would need to ship the typewriter to this location for "in-warranty" servicing.

As it happened, Mary Ann's typewriter required servicing for a plastic part that simply disintegrated after two years. The part cost a few dollars, not worth shipping a heavy machine two hundred miles. She had the machine serviced locally and paid the $17.50 labor charge to replace the part. Mary Ann decided to read the guarantee more carefully the next time she bought something.

Some guarantees fully protect you on the initial purchase, should you be unhappy for any reason with it. They may say, "Satisfaction guaranteed or your money refunded if merchandise is returned within fifteen days." But you usually have to pay the shipping charges both ways. What the merchandise is guaranteed to do or how well the product will hold up beyond the initial fifteen days may be another matter. You may need more than fifteen days to know whether the product is satisfactory.

According to the Federal Trade Commission, "The word *guarantee*, or *warranty*, is incomplete unless it is used in connection with other explanatory words. To say a product or other subject is guaranteed is meaningless."

Bob, sixteen, angrily told a lawyer, "I bought a bike for $120, and several days later the brake cable broke. I took it back to the dealer since it was in warranty, but they charged me six dollars to fix it."

Kerry, fifteen, complained, "I paid good money for a Labrador retriever that was guaranteed to have all the shots he needed for disease prevention. Whey my dog got terribly sick, the vet told me it hadn't had any shots at all."

Both young people had legitimate complaints. Bob hadn't fully understood that his guarantee didn't include labor charges, and Kerry had no written guarantee on his dog.

Just what is the guarantee? A guarantee should fully and clearly state:

1. What product or part of the product is guaranteed.

2. What duration does the guarantee include.

3. What the consumer, or anyone claiming rights under the guarantee, must do before the guarantor will fulfill his obligation (such as return the product, service only with authorized dealer, pay labor charges, etc.).

4. Who is the guarantor (the full identity of who guarantees this product or service).

5. How will the guarantee be carried out (replacement, refund, or repair), or whether the consumer has any choice in how the guarantee will be fulfilled.

Often a guarantor will make an adjustment by prorating the amount of time the consumer has used the product. For example, tires, batteries, and appliances may be considered to last a certain number of years normally. If you use the product for one half of that life-span, you may be entitled only to a price adjustment to buy another one. Such prorata adjustment should be clearly stated on the guarantee.

The time to understand the guarantee is *before* you buy something. Don't wait until you have used a product or found a defect to read the guarantee. Understand fully before you buy what the warranty does and does not cover, and who will make good on the product if it is partly defective. One industry organization recommended that if a consumer has an identical problem with a product repeatedly during the warranty period, the warranty should be extended or the product replaced. However, the recommendation is not often put in practice.

"Lifetime guarantees" may not be worth much when the product life-span is not defined, or when the company no longer exists five years after you've bought an expensive set of cookware. Know the company from which you buy.

Advertisements often try to lure you to buy based on "guaranteed savings." Have you ever seen an ad that said, "Guaranteed to save you 50 percent," or "Guaranteed lowest price in town"? Have you wondered 50 percent of what? If a store guarantees that they sell at the lowest price in town, will they cut their price if another store legitimately sells at a lower price? If an ad says, "Guaranteed to trim your waist or your money back," this claim represents that the product will actually do so and should not be used in an ad unless the product is capable of slimming your waist, says the Federal Trade Commission.

There are many types of guarantees, including: unconditional guarantees; parts and labor under normal use; parts but not labor. If you have an unconditional guarantee, the seller will take back your purchase for any reason. You may have found a lower price elsewhere; you may decide you don't really need or like what you bought. Usually you must return the merchandise within ten days, with sales slip included, and the goods must not be used. Most department stores will allow such exchanges, and major mail-order houses are quite fair about returns even when the goods have been used if they are for some reason unsatisfactory.

A parts-and-labor guarantee under normal use is a guarantee that usually applies for a short period of time, say thirty to ninety days. If you have abused the goods, the guarantee may not apply. Sometimes a service charge is made to repair such merchandise. With inexpensive cameras and watches, for example, the service charge may be almost as much as a new item.

If parts but not labor are covered by your guarantee, you may find yourself with a substantial bill. As with Mary Ann's typewriter, with television sets, and digital clock radios, the parts often cost very little. The work to replace the part is much more expensive. Find out what you are getting for your guarantee.

A verbal guarantee is usually worthless. Don't mistake sales talk for a real guarantee. In the courts, it is called "puffing" and is not the same as a warranty. A salesman may say, "This is a great little car," but he is not making a specific promise. If he does, get it in writing to be sure it is valid.

Small-Claims Court

While no one expects a layman, adult, or teen-ager to have complete knowledge of the law, everyone should be acquainted with some of the basics so that he knows where to turn for help in case of trouble. Small-claims court is one facet of the law the consumer should know about. It offers a fast, fair, cheap, and simple system of justice in which you don't need a lawyer. In fact, in most cases, you aren't allowed to have one. Some people call small claims a "do-it-yourself justice system." Not quite. But for the vast majority who bring a case to small-claims court, this system delivers justice with a minimum of time and money invested.

Who can sue in small-claims court? Anyone, although in some states if the defendant is under eighteen, a "friend in court" must be appointed to represent his interests.

What does it cost and what kind of cases come to these courts? To bring action, you pay a one-dollar filing fee in advance, and other fees may bring the total to five dollars. Claims are made by consumers who seek damages on defective merchandise and people who have suffered property damage or personal injury under five hundred dollars (three hundred dollars in some states). Creditors may sue on unpaid bills.

How do you file a claim? Scott, seventeen, tried repeatedly to get XYZ Auto Repair Shop to give satisfaction on a carburetor they claimed to have fixed. He was charged sixty-five dollars, but he felt sure the work was never done. He wrote letters, made phone calls, and finally filed a claim with the small-claims court. Scott went to his local courthouse and filled out a work sheet to aid the clerk in preparing his claim form. Scott (the plaintiff) paid his one-dollar filing fee and was told that his case would be heard within a few weeks. The XYZ Auto Repair Shop (called the defendant) received notice of the claim by registered mail a few days later. Scott got a phone call to bring his car in for reservicing, and the claim was settled without a court appearance.

Work Sheet for Filing a Small Claim

PLAINTIFF'S STATEMENT TO CLERK	**THURSTON COUNTY DISTRICT COURT** Thurston County, State of Washington Olympia, Washington 98501	Case Number

1. Please read carefully the instructions appearing below before filling out this form:
   a. If you are suing one or more individuals, give full name of each.
   b. If you are suing a business owned by an individual, give the name of the owner and the name of the business he owns.
   c. If you are suing a partnership, give the names of the partners and the name of the partnership.
   d. If you are suing a corporation, give its full name.
   e. If your claim arises out of a vehicle accident, the **driver** of the other vehicle must be named, and the registered owner of the other vehicle should also be named.

2. State your name and residence address, and the name and address of any other person joining with you in this action. If this claim arises from a business transaction, give the name and address of your business.
   a. Name _____
      Address _____ Phone No. _____
   b. Name _____
      Address _____ Phone No. _____

3. State the name and address of each person or business firm you are suing:
   a. Name _____
      Address _____
   b. Name _____
      Address _____
   c. Name _____
      Address _____

4. State the amount you are claiming. $ _____

5. Describe **briefly** the nature of your claim: _____
   _____
   _____
   _____

6. Fill out this section **if your claim arises out of a vehicle accident:**
   a. Date on which accident occurred: _____, 19___
   b. Street or intersection and city or locality where accident occurred:
   _____
   c. If you are claiming damages to a vehicle, were you on the date of the accident the registered owner of that vehicle? _____
      (yes or no)

7. If your claim does not arise out of a vehicle accident, give address below where obligation was entered into or was to be performed or where injury was incurred.
   _____
   (street address)   (city or locality)

8. I have received and read the form entitled "Information to Plaintiff".

   _____
   Signature

Notice of Small Claim

THURSTON COUNTY DISTRICT COURT
Thurston County, State of Washington
Olympia, Washington 98501

Plaintiff (name)

Address - phone number

Defendant (name)

No. _____

NOTICE OF SMALL CLAIM

Address - phone number

STATE OF WASHINGTON
County of Thurston } ss.

To the Above Named Defendant:

You are hereby notified to be and appear at the Court Room of the said Court, Room 203, Thurston County Court House, Olympia, Washington on the _____ day of _____, 19____, at the hour of ____ o'clock __.M., to answer the foregoing Complaint, or judgment will be taken against you as confessed, and the prayer of the plaintiff granted.

By: _____

Deputy Clerk

SMALL CLAIM

The above mentioned plaintiff alleges that the above named defendant is indebted to the above named plaintiff in the sum of $ _____ for _____

_____

(auto damages, wages, rent, loan, goods, etc.)

and that the plaintiff has made demand upon the defendant and that defendant refuses to pay same.

The plaintiff prays for judgment against the defendant as alleged above, plus court costs.

Subscribed and sworn before me this _____ day of _____, 19____

Plaintiff _____

REGISTRY			
Date	Rec'd.	Disbursed	Rec't. No.

Deputy Clerk

Case dismissed by Plaintiff with ☐ without ☐ prejudice.

What else could the defendant do? If the accused did not wish to settle out of court, he could make no appearance at the trial, thus allowing the plaintiff to win his claim by default. Or he may appear to present his side of the case.

What happens at a small-claims court hearing? Each person explains to the judge his side of the case. If you sue in a small-claims court, you should go well prepared to present your story, with any evidence that applies. You should have receipts, notes, checks, and a small notebook with any information you feel is important to your case. The judge will ask questions and will either announce his decision right then, or he will tell you that you will be notified by mail of his decision. If you win your case, you receive a judgment, a piece of paper that says you have the right to collect. If the defendant doesn't pay promptly, you may go to a collection agency or serve a writ of garnishment on the defendant's bank or employment. This writ requires the bank or employer to tell the court the amount of money it is holding for that person, and the court can then require the money to be paid into a court registry for you.

Often just knowing how well protected you are as a consumer is an extremely effective weapon. For instance, in some states new laws have been made to protect the consumer from being cheated. In Washington State a law called RCW 1986 describes remedies available to the consumer. If a dry cleaner ruins your leather coat that cost $300, you may sue for up to three times the actual cost. This suit must be made through a private attorney, and the cost must not exceed $1,000. If you have this weapon in hand, chances are you'll get quick and easy recovery of damages from a firm anxious to avoid additional court and attorney fees.

Even though your principal purchases for the moment are probably clothes, bikes, stereos, and sports gear, you will be buying far larger things soon, from cars and college education to apartments and investments. You will be dealing with the law of our land all your life. Why not begin as a teen-ager to understand your legal rights and responsibilities, both as a citizen and as a consumer?

Complaints are many and various.
ROBERT GRAVES

9

Don't Complain for Practice

Did you ever buy something that proved defective all too soon after you bought it? What did you do about it? All of us have probably had the experience of putting up with the defect, repairing it ourselves, or we may have discarded the product long before its expected lifetime.

I once began to think a little black cloud hovered over everything I bought. The troubles began with a shiny new station wagon whose air-conditioning unit copped out the day we planned to leave for summer vacation. My series of defects continued with uneasy regularity that summer. I look back at one incident. I saw an expensive golf skirt early in the summer, and when it was marked down in August, I bought it for twenty dollars—still a high price for a pants skirt. The fabric tag claimed the skirt was 100 percent polyester, machine washable. The short skirt was white, with navy polka-dotted shorts underneath. On the first washing, the skirt came through beautifully, but the shorts shriveled up to two thirds their original size. Instead of trim-fitting shorts, I now had brief, wide

145

ones. I casually mentioned the problem to the store where I had purchased them, but no offer of adjustment was made. I kept the skirt, now no longer suitable for any use but backyard gardening. The experience was not wasted, though. Every time I wear the twenty-dollar "bargain," I am reminded not to let myself be disappointed again. I have since learned how to complain effectively with a minimum of frustration and effort. By following five simple rules, you can gnash through the red tape, save money, and solve many of your consumer problems.

1. Don't tell your story for practice. When you have a problem that you feel you shouldn't have in the first place, few things are harder on self-control than to refrain from telling the story to friends and family over and over. Save yourself a lot of misery (and your friends) by finding someone who can help you with the problem.

First call the store and ask for the person in charge. Once you have the right person on the line, tell him why you are dissatisfied.

2. Don't lose your temper. Learn to complain effectively. Ranting and raving may ease your mind for a moment, but in the long run anger will get you nowhere. If you blow your cool, your attitude will only antagonize your listener. Stick to the facts. Have your sales slip, receipt, or copy of any agreement, warranty or ad that you feel misrepresented the sale.

State your problem clearly and as concisely as possible. Don't get off track and talk about other things that aren't relevant to this problem.

You can learn to be your own consumer advocate by handling problems yourself rather than asking your parents to take care of returning defective merchandise. Mike, sixteen, bought inexpensive wood skis from J.C. Penney. His first time down the slope one ski

broke in two. A neighbor, an experienced skier, looked at the skis and determined that both skis were warped, which may have helped cause the ski to break. Metal edges also appeared to have pulled away from one ski. Mike decided to return the skis and ask for an adjustment. He took the sales slip, along with both skis, then asked to see the department manager. "I bought these skis ten days ago," he began calmly. "On my first run down the hill, one of them broke." He showed the ski. "I wonder if they could be defective, since they seem to be warped." Mike hoped for a replacement of the one ski or for a partial refund. He also realized that any wood ski could break readily.

The sales manager recalled the purchase, since he had also fitted Mike with ski boots and bindings. Since the store didn't have other identical skis in stock, Mike got a full refund. Had he gone into the store hopping mad, he might not have been treated as well.

Most stores are anxious to maintain customer goodwill. Since Mike's ski purchase was on his parents' charge account, a few days later they received a letter of inquiry asking how their complaint transaction was handled, and if they were satisfied with the adjustment.

3. Don't be afraid to speak out. As I write, I recall the casual mention I made of the golf-skirt problem. Had I been more forceful, making a direct effort to get an adjustment, I feel sure that I could have saved myself some money—and some hostility, too. Communication between consumers and manufacturers is needed. Very likely, the store would have returned the merchandise to the manufacturer, who would then realize that something went wrong with this garment. I should have emphasized that I bought the skirt because it was labeled machine washable, that I had indeed followed washing directions, using warm water. Recognizing mistakes would be more profitable for the businessman than losing my business or the trade of anyone I could influence.

If you are too nice to complain, you do yourself and the business a disfavor. If no one knows you're unhappy, you'll never get anything accomplished in the marketplace. Effective complaining is an important part of getting the most for your money.

4. Don't let distance stop you. Suppose the company that made your product isn't in your city. Well, take your pen in hand (or typewriter if you can) and begin to think through your presentation. You'll have time to rework and polish your letter, to state your case as effectively as possible. To whom do you write? Try your best to get in touch with the right man, the head of customer service, service manager, or perhaps the president of the company, depending on the problem you have. You can get the address of major companies, as well as the president's name, by calling the reference department of the library or by checking in *Poor's Register of Corporations, Directors and Executives* at the library.

When you write, keep the letter short and to the point. Simply state your problem, tell your efforts to get it solved, and ask for help. State what you wish the company to do about your problem. Thank him for his attention and end the letter.

Do you think letters really work? Indeed they do. Here are two examples: Steve, fourteen, sent a check to a record club with his order for two expensive albums. Four months later the records had not yet arrived, in spite of two letters he had written to the company asking about them. He wrote another letter, this time threatening to take legal action. Here's what Steve wrote in his third letter.

Dear Sirs:

My record club account number is MC 8098. On September 10, I sent a check number 365, written by my mother, Ellen Jones, in full payment for two record albums listed in your monthly news. The records I ordered were *The Best of the Guess Who* and *Neil Diamond Gold*. The check was cashed on October 12, but I have not yet received my records. I have written two previous letters. In the past, my account has been handled satisfactorily, but at this time I am getting disgusted with your record club.

I have today filed a complaint against you with the Office of the Attorney General for the State of Washington. If I do not hear from you within ten days, I shall be forced to take stronger action.

Steve received a check plus a letter of apology a week later.

Here's another instance where writing to the top brass in a company unraveled a tangled credit-card mess. Scott, a young executive, on a business trip, tried to pay his rental-car bill with a major credit card. The clerk seemed to take an unusual amount of time to process the charge slip. When she returned to the counter, she said, "I'm sorry, sir, but we'll have to pick up your card. Your account is apparently long overdue." Scott was furious and extremely embarrassed. When he arrived home, he checked his bills and his checkbook to determine when that account was last paid. The last statement he had received from that company appeared to be six months ago, and he had paid it in full.

He immediately called the library, got the address of the president of the credit-card company, and fired off a forceful letter giving the facts of his case. He received a quick note of apology, plus a promise to have the matter investigated. The company apparently had an old address for Scott and had never changed its records to show his new address. When the post office no longer forwarded mail from the old address, the bills were returned to the credit company undelivered. They had made no effort to locate his new address. His bill mounted up from business travel over a six-month period. A new bill was sent to him, including over sixty dollars in interest charges, to compound the insult. Scott asked for Xeroxed copies of all his charges for the period of time he had not received bills. He then received, along with his own charge slips, several charges made to another account, with a name not at all similar to his. Once again Scott wrote to the manager handling his account, *with a carbon copy to the president.* In short order, the matter was resolved, the interest charges dropped, and Scott was urged to continue his account with the company.

5. Never lose confidence in your ability to win. If you have a justifiable complaint, your chance of having a satisfying result depends largely on your ability to prove your case. If the chips are down, the person you are trying to convince won't budge, remember that you alone hold the ultimate weapon. You can complain to every possible agency that might apply to your case, from the State Consumer Protection Office to the newspaper that carried an ad for the product. As Steve did with his record-club problem, you can contact the Attorney General's Office, or you can take the case to small-claims court, depending on the extent of your problem. Sometimes you have to wage an all-out war with a company to get satisfaction. Every honest and effective complaint, though, makes the next consumer transaction easier.

Don't complain when you simply change your mind about something you've bought, or when you find you can get a better deal elsewhere, or when no misrepresentation has been made. Shop and compare *before* you buy.

Many stores, however, do give you the right to change your mind about a purchase even if there's nothing wrong with it. If something doesn't suit you as well when you get it home as you thought it did in the store, you can usually return it, provided you haven't worn it. To do so, you should have the sales slip, the tags should be on the merchandise, and you should contact the store within a week after purchase. Some stores will refund your money, while others will give a credit voucher for another purchase. Bathing suits, underwear, and sale items are not returnable, but you are usually advised of this fact before you buy.

Where to Begin

Suppose you are perfectly happy with your purchase, but something goes wrong. The stereo stops working properly, or the brake on your ten-speed doesn't function. Even though the item may not be covered by a written guarantee, you have the right to expect reasonable service through implied warranty. Don't pay for repairs yourself or discard something, if you feel the problem is caused by a defect and not normal wear and tear. If you haven't abused the product, go back to the store where you bought it. When you enter the store, ask immediately for customer service or for the store manager. If you do not have a sales slip, ask the clerk to have the merchandise tagged as a return to remove any suspicion that you have shoplifted the item. If the merchandise is clothing, tell why you want to return it, and be sure to state whether you have laundered it according to directions.

Many stores will send the defective merchandise back to the company and give you a new item. Others will send your purchase back for servicing, and you must wait for it to be repaired. Still others may take no responsibility and advise you to send the product to the manufacturer or to an authorized service center. If you deal with a reputable firm, you stand a good chance of getting satisfaction if a product is not satisfactory for any reason.

Suppose you fail the first time you try to get an adjustment on a product or on some service? Well, there's not much to be lost by making another attempt. For example, Patti went to a department-store beauty salon for a "body permanent" for her long blonde hair. Her hair was sun streaked, but had never been commercially color treated. The store insisted on giving her a mild permanent prepared for bleached hair, more expensive than a regular permanent. Four days later Patti returned to the salon to show the manager that indeed she had no body to her hair. It was as fine as ever, poker straight, and she had paid twenty dollars. After much discussion, the shop wet her hair, agreed there was no permanent in it, shampooed it, and used a hot comb to blow her hair dry. They charged Patti another four dollars and told her to come back in six months when they "might be able to use a stronger permanent on your hair." The salon manager gave Patti a card saying she could get the new permanent at half price. Nearly in tears, Patti could scarcely talk she was so angry. Her hard-earned car-hop money was spent, and her hair was still as limp as ever.

A few days later, when Patti felt more in control of the situation, she phoned the store manager to tell her story. She was given a twenty-dollar refund, enough to find another salon to do her hair.

Special Channels for Complaints

Many states now have a Consumer Hotline, a telephone number you can call toll free to aid in consumer problems. When Steve began to track down his record problems, he first called the Washington State Consumer Hotline. (You can get the phone number by dialing directory assistance, if you can't locate it in the phone book.) The Hotline advised Steve to write to the Attorney General's Office and give all the facts about his case. A consumer adviser can tell you where to turn in your problems and what legal recourse you have.

Newspapers, radio stations, and television stations also have consumer-action columns and programs. Try one of them for action if you seem to be batting zero with a problem.

One of the most effective quick-action efforts many consumers have found is to tell the store they will complain to the newspaper in which the product was advertised. Rick went to a store, ad in hand, to buy sale-priced walkie-talkies. When he got there, a clerk said they had not yet received the shipment on the walkie-talkies, and he would have to come back in a few days. Rick had the uneasy feeling that if he came back, the merchandise would be sold out. He asked to see the manager. "Please don't advertise something you don't have," Rick began. "I intend to call the *Herald*, which ran this ad. I made a special trip here to buy these." "Let me see if they're among the boxes not unpacked yet," the manager offered, "and if not, we'll give you a voucher for them." Oddly enough, Rick left the store with his sale-priced walkie-talkies in hand, even though the first store clerk made little effort to help him.

The Better Business Bureau, known as BBB, is another possible place to complain about unfair business practices. However, BBB is an organization of established businessmen, and you may not get much help, unless the firm you complain about is a nonmember. Often the BBB will only say, "We have no record of complaints against them." Your local Chamber of Commerce may also be an effective channel to complain through.

If you have a complaint about any food, drug, cosmetic, or medical device that you feel is mislabeled, or in anyway harmful, you will be doing a public service by reporting it to the Food and Drug Administration, 5600 Fishers Lane, Rockville, Maryland 20852, or to the office nearest you. Check your phone book for a listing under United States Government, Department of Health, Education and Welfare, Food and Drug Administration. Before you complain, though, ask yourself a few questions: Did I use the product as labeled? Did I follow the instructions carefully? Was the product old when I opened it? If you have an unusual reaction from a medicine, it could be an allergy or side effect and should be reported to your doctor first.

Report any problems as quickly as possible after they occur. Give your name, address, and phone number, as well as directions on how to get to your home. State clearly what you feel is wrong, and describe in detail the product label. Save whatever remains of the product. For example, save the can that contained contaminated food, since code markings are usually embossed on the lid. Give the name, address of the store where purchased, and date of purchase. Also report any problem to the store where you bought it and to the manufacturer or distributor shown on the label.

Other government agencies you may complain to for specific problems include the following:

Possible false advertising:
  Federal Trade Commission
Suspected sale of narcotics or dangerous drugs:
  Drug Enforcement Administration
  United States Department of Justice
Unsolicited or pornographic mail:
  United States Postal Service
Hazardous toys or household products:
  Consumer Product Safety Commission
Discrimination:
  Human Rights Commission

Many states have now set up consumer-protection offices, some as part of the Attorney General's Office, others as separate departments within the state government. When the state office investigates a problem, a large majority of firms make prompt adjustment. If the consumer-protection division gets the same complaint about a firm from many consumers, a pattern of illegal practices may be detected and the office could then file a lawsuit against a firm. In individual cases, though, that office has no authority to force adjustments.

You can also resort to the small-claims court, as outlined in chapter eight.

Many consumer organizations exist to help citizens band together with an effective voice in the marketplace. Some of them state their purpose as "pressing to make government respond to the needs of citizens," while others explore in depth the most pressing consumer problems or try to awaken consumer concern. Consumer organizations include: National Consumers League; Consumer Federation of America; Common Cause; Consumer Interests Foundation; Consumer Help Center, sponsored by George Washington Law School, staffed by students. You can find the address and summary of purpose for these groups by asking at a library for the *Encyclopedia of Associations.*

Follow the suggestions given here, and you will find being your own consumer advocate isn't so hard after all. Be persistent and if your cause is just, most cases will turn out in your favor. Remember that everyone makes mistakes, so keep your sense of humor as you complain. Don't lose your cool. Give the seller a chance to save face as he makes amends.

To be sure, young adults have tremendous influence in the marketplace. A University of Texas research study said that the average teen-age girl's disposable income is more than that of most people who live in a $40,000 home. Although teens spend about twenty-four billion dollars a year, they influence the spending of four times that amount.

Yet before the mid-seventies, few young people were given any guidance at all in how to get sound value for their dollar. Most were unaware of the tremendous resources that exist to help them learn to use money wisely. Dan Jones, nineteen, wrote to his high-school principal in Washington State. "I graduated last year with good grades in all the academic courses. Yet how much of what I learned can I put to practical use in my life now—or five years from now? Why didn't you teach me something about the financial facts of life —about borrowing money, banking, buying on credit, or even how to budget?"

Many other students have said much the same thing. Consumer education has become an urgent need. Even very young students take interest in understanding the complexities of advertising. A third-grade class in Euclid, Ohio, analyzed television commercials, then wrote this one: "Woof—the only food your dog will ask for by name!"

If you have any doubts about the value of good consumer education in the teen years, remember this piece of advice: You can use it now, and you *can* take it with you.

Index

indicates illustration